Unspeakable Joy

Unspeakable Joy

a memoir

Connie Reemtsma

To honor my grandmother: Hwie Nio

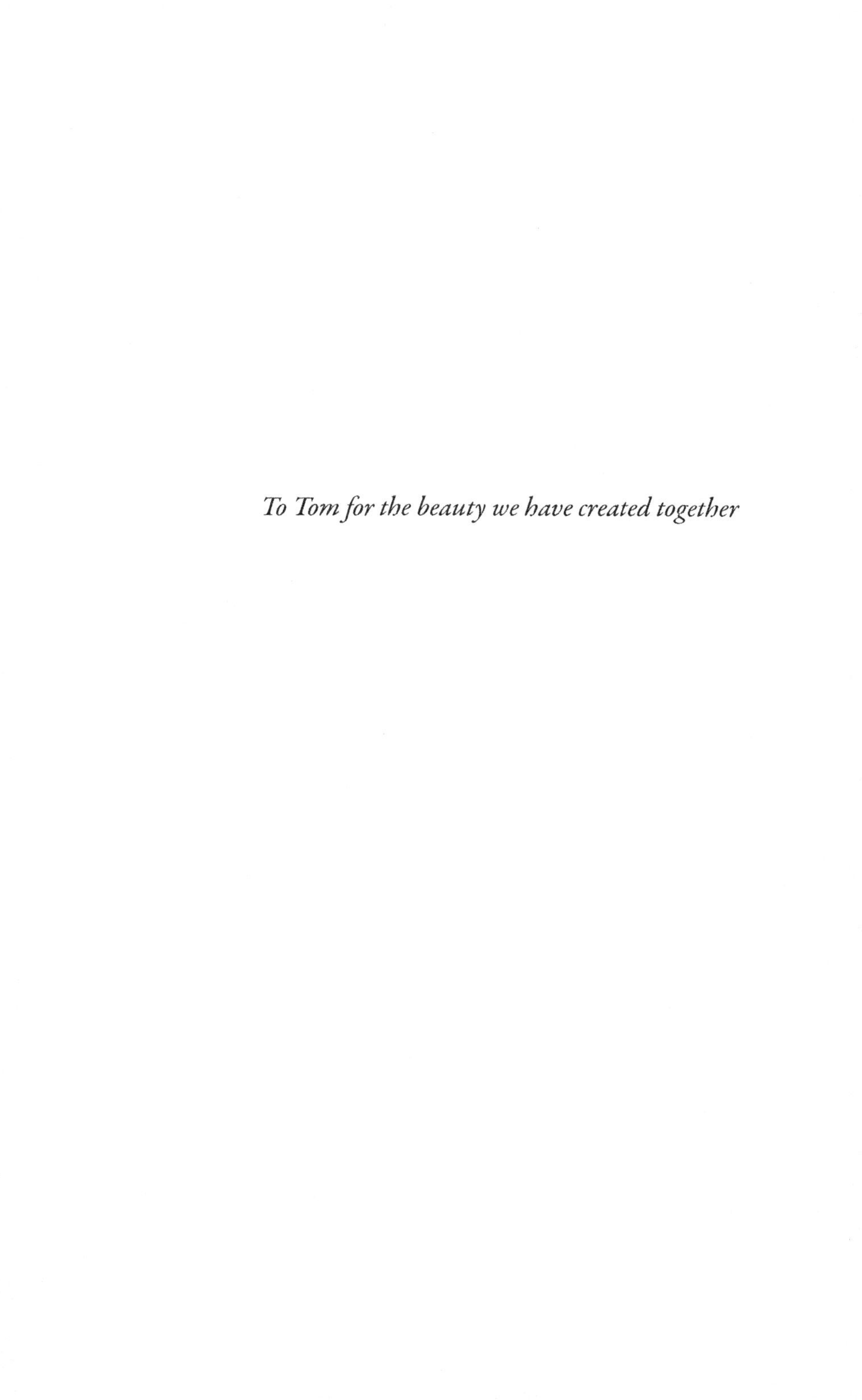

To Tom for the beauty we have created together

For the children and grandchildren of Valerie & Maud

If I speak with human eloquence and angelic ecstasy and don't love,
I'm nothing but the creaking of a rusty gate.
... No matter what I say, what I believe, and what I do,
I'm bankrupt without love.

1 Corinthians 13:1
The Message

Prelude

Urania invites to write pantoum.
A long time ago she persuades.
Only until I'm here in the desert
do I heed her call and write.

She persuades to remember the stars
on Indonesia's dark blue sky.
I write about Grandma's nutmeg tree,
my travels, encounters and yearnings.

Stars on a dark blue sky trigger memories
of Grandma's passion, discipline, and life goal.
Oh, how much I yearn for a center to call it mine.
For many years I am a stranger to myself.

Grandma's passion, discipline I trust on the path
of discovery to the center of my own.
I befriend the stranger within I do not know,
understand the tree and kittens in my dreams.

Other countries and cultures too I discover,
that enables to accept and respect my own self.
Kittens, the feminine need not be feared, but accepted.
Images of life giving energies, of great value.

To accept myself, I learn to respect the stranger.
Freed from bondages that held me back, I create.
Released life-giving energies help me find
my place and role as part of the whole.

At eighty, finally free, I wish to publish my memoir.
Aborted I reflect and be my own mentor.
Here in the desert as part of the whole I listen
and meet the underlying mystery of creation.

In self-mentoring I face the challenge of growth.
Grateful for the strength of love that sets me free.
I learn to love the underlying mystery of creation,
the rejected, the stranger, the unknown.

The love that sets me free, calls … to be who I am.
Only until I'm here in the desert,
I take up the challenge to find unspeakable joy.
Urania invites to write pantoum.

Chapter One

Among all the people in my extended family it was my maternal grandmother, Hwie Nio (pronounced as we nyo) who fascinated me most. I loved to look at her fine, oval face. Grandma was a beautiful woman with a stern, fearless, self-confident expression—her long, dark brown hair pulled to the back of her head, tied in a round knot, and fastened with a golden pin.

In Salatiga, a small town in central Java, Indonesia, she was known as "the lady under the nutmeg tree." Between her house and the bakery stood a huge, shady nutmeg tree, the only tree on the street. Large tiles were laid around its base. A hole in the trunk—about a third of its height above the ground—attracted nesting sparrows. One day when playing hide and seek with my sisters, Valerie and Maud, I peeked into the hole of the tree to find a freshly built nest holding three baby birds. In an effort to protect her young, the mother bird frantically flew around the opening of the hole. She was very disturbed. That scene of the mother bird protecting her babies stayed with me for a long time. This woke a yearning in me for an unknown, yet warm and safe space.

Behind the tree was a long cement breeze-blocked road that separated the house from the bakery. An iron gate marked the entrance from the road into the property. Five yards from the entrance was a strong wooden second gate. A few yards further on were three steps that led to the entrance into the bakery. Four bakers wore white hats and aprons, clothing they would rather not wear in the tropics, but prerequisites for a licensed bakery.

Grandma's workspace consisted of a large wooden table, a stool, a rack with an old fashion scale, and small card recipe boxes. A single dove in a cage hung over the balustrade between Grandma's workspace and her bedroom window. Grandma and Dara the dove woke at the very same time every morning. They enjoyed one another's company and seemed to encourage the other to face the day as it came, regardless of how ordinary life could be.

My sister Valerie and Grandma shared a bedroom. Occasionally I would sneak into Valerie's bed for the night and watch Grandma as she started and ended the day. Grandma had a beige metal bed with four poles. An elegant mosquito net with a ruffled layer of lace around the top covered the whole bed. A yard-long bundle of dried reeds about an inch thick lay at the foot of the bed. It looked like a short-handled witch's broom and was used as a swatter and to straighten the bed sheet. If a stubborn mosquito sneaked under the net, Grandma had her weapon to get rid of it.

Her alarm clock rang around four o'clock in the morning. She got up and listened for the morning shift baker to arrive who was let in by the evening shift baker. Then, sitting on her knees on the bed under the net, she'd say her morning prayers. Never did she forget reading a few Bible verses. After prayers and making her bed, she hooked both sides of the net into two golden colored loops and bathed.

Dressed in one of her favorite *sarongs* and *kebayas*, she looked stunning.1 By five in the morning she was dressed and ready for work. A hot cup of tea concluded her morning ritual.

At nine o'clock Aunt Willie, Grandma's niece who lived with her, opened the shop. Grandma had made sure everything was ready for her customers. At midmorning, four young women arrived to collect and sell her steamed and deep-fried snacks. Each of them carried a stack of four round tins on their backs in a kind of shawl, just like the way mothers carried their babies and toddlers. By noon the smell of freshly baked bread filled the bakery and its

---

1 A sarong is an Indonesian batik wrap-around skirt and a kebaya is a long sleeved blouse with an open front fastened with three fancy safety pins.

surroundings. The aroma made a person hungry for freshly baked raisin cinnamon breads and banana rolls. Around that time two men on bikes would arrive to pick up breads, rolls, and cakes. They displayed them in square tin boxes and vended them to the far-reaching areas. By five all the vendors returned to see Grandma for accountability. They checked in for goods sold and returned and received their earnings for a day's work. Then came the fun part of adding up all that the six vendors and Aunt Willie had brought in. Grandma loved sorting out the bills and coins, and recording the daily income.

Grandma then cooked her favorite dish as an addition to the cook's daily menu. She then refreshed herself with an Indonesian splashy bath and crisp clean clothes. She called all of us to the dining table for a meal. Grandma rarely skipped reading aloud a passage from the Bible followed by a prayer of praise and gratitude for the day.

She continued to do more chores for an hour or so while a maid chased the mosquitoes away and got the net hung neatly for the night. She always found a mosquito-free bed to retire in. To end the day she sat again on her knees and said her personal evening prayer.

Grandma was a disciplined person of determination and strong will power. She was a proud woman with many accomplishments. Single-handedly she has turned a small home baking effort into a fully licensed bakery. Then she invited her closest relatives, including her daughters and granddaughters to help achieve her goal in life: to put her only son, my Uncle Tiong, through medical school so she could count on him to provide and care for her in her older days—a spoken or an unspoken dream that most mothers had at that time. Uncle Tiong became a successful general practitioner in private practice. His marriage to a lady of a higher rank in the Dutch East Indies stratification brought not only him but also Grandma more respect and honor in society. Several years before he and his family immigrated to the Netherlands, he was director of a missionary hospital in Semarang, Central Java. He was indeed Grandma's dream come true: a respected provider of social security, medical care, and her life long personal physician.

What about her two daughters, my mother, Thio Som Nio and Aunt Ellie? How did she relate to them? She loved them very much too, but in a different way. Grandma's dream for her two daughters was to catch handsome, wealthy, ambitious husbands.

Multatuli, a Dutch novelist, described Indonesia (then the Dutch East Indies) as *De Gordel van Smaragd* (The Emerald Girdle) for its beauty and the vastness of the clusters of islands along the equator. Throughout the year it is always green everywhere you look. Its rice fields and plantations always held the promise for a great harvest. Since the sixteenth century, it has attracted Europeans seeking to monopolize its resources of valuable spices such as nutmeg, cloves, and pepper. The Dutch exploitation of Indonesian resources began in 1830 when the Netherlands was at the brink of bankruptcy. An agricultural policy of government-controlled forced cultivation, known as the *Cultuurstelsel* (Culture System), was introduced to Java. Much of Java became Dutch plantations and developed into a profitable, self-sufficient colony that saved the Netherlands from bankruptcy.

About the same time immigrations of ethnic Chinese traders, merchants, and laborers came into Southeast Asia—particularly into Indonesia. There were three waves of Chinese immigrations: the first was spurred by trading activities in the early fifteenth century, the second during the two Opium Wars in the nineteenth century, and the third was during the first half of the twentieth century due to the worsening economy during the Warlords Period.

Primarily, the Chinese immigrants hoped to find new trade opportunities in the Dutch East Indies. Some scholars pointed out that the earlier leaders of those voyages had also built Chinese Muslim communities along the shores of Java. Some of the earliest Islamic evangelists in Java,

Wali Songo (Nine Ambassadors) were of Chinese ancestry. *Masjid Agung Demak* (Great Demak Mosque), North East of Semarang, where my maternal grandfather—Grandma Hwie Nio's husband—was born and grew up, is one of the oldest mosques in Indonesia. It was built by Sunan Kalijaga, one of the Wali Songo group. I did not know grandpa that well. He was a kind man. The only thing I remembered of him was that one evening he took Valerie and I out for a walk. Grandpa had both of us hanging on each side of his arms and lifted us up in the air as we crossed a driveway. That was so much fun. He died young and left Grandma a young widow with two daughters, a son, and a bakery.

Chinese-Indonesians were those whose ancestors emigrated in the first and second waves from China, intermarried with the native Indonesian people, and assimilated into the culture. There was greater opportunity to obtain higher education and social status for those who identified themselves with the Dutch. Embracing Christianity and assimilating Western lifestyles was very appealing to the Chinese. Hardworking and ambitious traders at heart they easily pleased their Dutch employers.

A sharp distinction developed between the Chinese speaking and the Dutch speaking Chinese. The Chinese speaking Chinese were regarded as barbaric for many reasons: the use of chopsticks instead of fork and spoon, having no western table manners; and above all: belching after a fine meal. Although Grandma loved to eat out of her fingers, she insisted that the rest of us ate the Dutch way with a fork and spoon. "That's what your mother wanted you to do," she used to say. "You must be brought up to fit in the ranks of the Dutch East Indies social ladder."

Then there was another dilemma: race relations between the Dutch-speaking Chinese and the Pribumi (native Indonesians). The Dutch system made it disadvantageous for the Dutch-speaking Chinese to assimilate into the native population. Assimilation meant being placed in the lowest class. Ethnic Chinese, Arabs, and other Orientals were members of the second state. The first state was reserved for Europeans.

In the late nineteenth century, most of the aristocratic families rapidly westernized, becoming some of the strongest proponents of colonial rule. The Dutch-speaking Chinese actively helped strengthen Dutch domination in the region. In return the Dutch government rewarded loyal individuals with political positions such as *Kapitein der Chinezen* (Captain of the Chinese) Grandma had several cousins who reached the rank of major or captain in the aristocracy. Having the favor of the Dutch and being considered diligent, intelligent, and capable of managing

Dutch plantations, many Dutch-speaking Chinese supported colonial rule.

Against the backdrop of these cultural, socio-political landscapes my mother was born and raised to be an ambitious businesswoman. In1901 Queen Wilhelmina, the Dutch reigning queen declared that the Ethical Policy must include the start of western education for indigenous children. One of the fortunate few indigenous children who completed western primary education was my mother.

After primary school she was obliged to stay home, as according to Grandma, girls were not privileged to continue into higher education. Instead, she received homeschooling in Dutch history and literature.

During that era the Dutch speaking Chinese could become intermediaries between the European merchants and the Javanese peasants. In order to become an intermediary one had to adopt the Dutch culture, which included a name change, maintaining a certain income, and sending their children to Dutch schools. Although Grandma, converted to Christianity and adopted the western lifestyle, my grandparents did not belong to that class. Grandma was acutely aware of Mother's dream to be a member of that class, but she could do nothing more to help her achieve this goal. Grandma resented my father's lack of enthusiasm for achievement that prevented Mother to reach her dream.

Mother at 35 in Salatiga

Their dreams were not the same. Mother might have considered working for advancement on her own, but single women, or women acting independently, were simply not accepted. Mother continued to dream. She became obsessed by this desire and pushed very hard in business all her life, but in doing so jeopardized her health. She envied the wealthy, well-travelled ladies who came to her bakery shop. These women had the most fascinating stories to tell about the Netherlands and England. At times their fascinating stories spurred a jealous desire for travel in Mother that made her so angry at life.

Mother's sister, Ellie, and her husband, Ping Tjwan (pronounced as Chuan), also lived at Grandma's big house. A year before Mother died, Aunt Ellie became pregnant. It was common in Indonesia at that time for any adult to adopt babies of relatives, based on a mutual agreement. Since Mother did not have any sons, she decided to adopt one. She tried to persuade Grandma to have Aunt Ellie agree that if her first-born was a boy Mother could adopt him. Considering that this was Aunt Ellie's first child, Grandma was unsure about such an outcome. Aunt Ellie gave birth to a stillborn son.

The following year Aunt Ellie gave birth to her second son, Djiang (pronounced as gee-aang). It was a joy to watch her breast-feed him. Both of them looked so happy together. Three years later came the twins, Tjong and An. They, too, were so welcomed by their parents. I envied them for having such a warm welcome to life. Occasionally, she let me hold them in my arms, or put them in the blue decorated cradle she had made months before they were born. Often, I felt that I was not one of Aunt Ellie's family unit, although we lived in the same house and were surrounded by the same people. In the midst of abundance, I didn't feel abundant—instead I felt empty, sad, and remorseful. As I grew older, I began to yearn to leave Grandmother's home and create my own, one where I would truly belong. At the age of thirteen, this desire to have my own home grew more intense. I identified and focused on a new goal: to be self-sufficient, yet remain a part of the extended family.

During the three years of Japanese occupation (1940-1942) only Maud, who was six years old, went to a public school. Out of fear of being molested or raped by aggressive, adventurous Japanese soldiers, Valerie (10) and I (9) received home tutoring in Dutch literature, history, math, and home economics. We were sheltered and kept inside the house, and were only allowed to go to Bible class chaperoned by an adult.

In 1945, President Sukarno proclaimed Indonesia's independence, setting off a four-year war before the Dutch formally recognized Indonesia's independence in 1949. This period of time was known as the Indonesian War of Independence. Simultaneously there was an internal social revolution—Dutch-loyalists and anti-Dutch-loyalists fought.

Local militias took advantage of the uncertain situation following the proclamation. During that time, Grandma, her family, and almost everyone in town were ordered to leave their homes with only an hour's notice. People were taken hostage in villages during the day, forced to walk during the night, and robbed of all belongings they had brought with them to exchange for food and safety. It took about ten days before relatives in nearby cities could finally come to their rescue and plead for their safety and return.

Valerie and I had been sent to stay with Grandma's brother and his family in Jogyakarta, 50 miles southwest of Salatiga, several weeks before that period of social upheaval. Valerie was called back home to help Grandma in the bakery. On the day I was to travel home, grandpa became ill. We postponed the trip, which allowed me to escape the tortuous nightmare. In one sense, I was grateful for being spared that horrifying experience, and in another, I had missed a strong and meaningful family and community-unifying event. Missing the forced march left me with a deep aching and longing for inclusion that has remained with me throughout my life.

Aunt Ellie had a reputation as a dressmaker and skillful fashion designer in town. She had a large international clientele. A Filipino woman and her New Zealander friend were regular customers. The others were Indonesian and

Dutch ladies. She always made sure Valerie, Maud, and I were well dressed. Even when Mother was still alive, Ellie was the one who sewed our dresses.

Like twins, Valerie and I wore the same style of dresses cut out of the same fabric. I was five years old; before I contracted the poliovirus.

When we were older we chose our own style, fabric,

and color. As an adolescent, very unsure about who I was and what I wanted, it was difficult for me to choose fabrics, colors, and styles. One day, Aunt Ellie took the three of us out to shop for materials in the large department stores of Semarang, Central Java's capital city. Valerie and Maud easily picked the fabrics they wanted, but nothing appealed to me. It was close to lunchtime and everybody was getting tired and hungry. Still undecided, I burst into tears and said to Aunt Ellie, "You really don't care about me. Do you? You only want me to be dressed in this cheap, ugly stuff! (In fact it was the best quality of fabric there was.) You like Valerie and Maud better than me because they are more agreeable and compliant with what you want." Aunt Ellie was hurt and embarrassed that I made such a scene at the store. It was a dreadful experience, hurting someone whom I most loved. This experience, and others similar to it, happened over and over again at the most unexpected moments, and the memories stayed with me for years. I felt rejected, but by whom?

Gradually, I learned to accept myself for my own thoughts, feelings, and for whom I proclaimed myself to be.

Aunt Ellie did not abandon me. Once we were preparing for a Christmas feast. My job was to get the meat out of about thirty crabs for Grandma's delicious asparagus crab soup. I loved the taste of thick and juicy crabmeat before it went into the soup and tasted more than a little. So I told Grandma that those were skinny crabs and therefore had less meat, and suggested that next time she buy larger and fatter crabs. Upon hearing what I said to Grandma, Aunt Ellie, who earlier had witnessed my crabmeat tasting episodes, giggled, and winked at me. She did not say a word to Grandma about what had happened. That became our secret.

Grandma's niece, Aunt Willie, lived with us. Aunt Willie, my sister Maud, and I shared a bedroom. During the day Aunt Willie helped Grandma in her bakery and shop. I could not say Aunt Willie was a friend. She liked to play the role of a watchdog.

One day, I came home from school with a library book about Florence Nightingale, *The Lady with the Lamp* (1820-1910); the story of an English nurse who tended injured soldiers during the Crimean War. Her life of determination, discipline, and rebellion against the social expectation of her time held me captive for many hours. I almost forgot to do my homework for the next day. I forgot to take a shower, was late for supper, and did not clean up my room. I finished reading the book before bedtime. Aunt Willie had reminded me several times to stop reading, but I ignored her warnings. When I finished,

I put the book on a chair, and headed for the bathroom. I saw her prepare to grab it. Before she reached it, I stepped back and picked it up. At that moment I hit her very lightly in the face. It all happened in just a split second and I was shocked and instantly regretted everything because I knew she would report the altercation to Grandma.

Grandma was very upset, especially because she was worried over what had happened the night before. About 9:00 pm, she heard the sound of a hardcover book falling from the top of my mother's bookcase to the floor. The next evening at 9:00 pm, again, she heard that same sound. Grandma asked all of us to gather in the main living room the following evening just before 9:00 pm, and to listen carefully. As requested, everybody was present. At the stroke of nine I heard the sound of a dropped book!

Grandma had strong suspicions about books. She thought that reading was an insult to the supremacy of daily human activities such as cooking, washing, and cleaning. "Reading has a bad influence on people," she said. "Besides it is unnatural for a child to curl up in a rattan chair reading the day away, while the adults work hard to earn a dime. She (referring to me) must learn how to earn a living by working hard, not by reading books. Reading derails people from the right track of living a good religious life. The only book a person should read is the Bible. Reading books makes one lazy, disobedient, and fills one with strange ideas," she continued.

As the 'The Lady with the Lamp' was an image of Florence Nightingale's conscious action against the expectation of society's elite in her time, so were books images of a consciousness that Grandma feared. I was touched by Nightingale's courage and deeply admired her going against the grain to bring about change in caring for the sick.

The next day, Grandma came up with the idea of burning Mother's books. She hired a man to carry all the books to the back yard, and had him burn a few books at a time until every single book turned into ashes. When I got home from school that day, I found the ashes of Mother's books under the banana trees in the backyard. I was astonished, very sad, and puzzled about the episode that had such a grip on Grandma. I did not dare to cry or ask Grandma why she did that horrible thing. The books were my only tangible and valuable remnant of my mother. I was also scared to do anything that might be considered evil that would separate me from God. Although those books were burned, the images of adventure, discovery, other cultures and philosophies live forever in my memory.

I always thought that Aunt Willie liked Maud much better than me, because Maud was more obedient to her than I. Still, at times, having Aunt Willie around was enjoyable. When it rained heavily with thunder and lightning at night, Maud and I liked to crawl closer together in Aunt Willie's bed until the storm was over. I hated her for being a watchdog, but at the same time I also appreciated her for being a big sister who provided us with a feeling of security and protection throughout stormy nights.

It was a part of my nature and heritage to hide any distress. No one must know what was going on inside my mind. One afternoon, after I had my third or fourth bath for the day, I put on clean, crispy underwear and my favorite white dress. I headed towards the front verandah with a book. I sat on the cool, white marble tiles. I slowly became aware of sitting in a puddle of blood. I was horrified. Aunt Willie walked by, became suspicious, and asked what I was trying to hide this time. She saw the book, but she sensed there was something else that I didn't tell her. I stood up, feeling unfamiliar fright. Aunt Willie saw the red mark on my dress, and instead of scolding, she hugged me. "Let's go inside and get you another dress, and I'll tell you a woman-to-woman secret. You are a grown-up woman now." Aunt Willie's words and calm demeanor instilled a welcome sense of relief. Above all, it gave me a sense of significance and recognition.

Chapter Two

One day Mother found me looking at a picture book with my nanny, mBok (Mrs.) Minah, sitting beside me. I was only seven years old. "Was she hired to read, while I am working hard to pay her?" she furiously asked. I knew I was not allowed to let a servant sit idly. She was hired to work for me: make my bed, tidy my desk and wardrobe, wash the tiled floor, and dust the windows and much more. It was my duty to keep her busy all the time. When there was nothing left to do for me she was to help elsewhere in the house. If at any time Mother found her not busy, I was to be blamed and no ice cream for the week was the punishment. Minah was illiterate and fascinated by how a book could tell stories. She also was as interested in me as Mother was in her business.

It was understood that a servant was not allowed to stand face-to-face with her/his boss, even if the boss was a child. So she always had to lower her body and approach me from the side when she wanted to talk to me. I thought that was an awkward position for her, as she was not only an adult, but also a heavy-built woman. Exceptions could be made when the super boss was not around, I thought.

So I allowed her do what was most convenient for her, risking a reprimand.

I learned the appropriate ways to treat servants at a young age. Whether I liked it or not, I was brought up to be bossy.

Obsessed with her strife to climb up the social ladder, Mother was determined to work harder and harder in her bakery and catering business. Despite her busy life, however, she made time to read. She loved novels, romance and European history books.

Occasionally there were very special events arranged for me. Minah gave me a *mandi* (pronounced as man-dee: a splashy, cool, shower) around five in the afternoon. She took me to a tiled bathroom with a small tub in one of the corners. The tub was always filled to the brim with cold water. She dipped a bowl into the water and poured it over me. The cool, splashing water felt very good and refreshing. She dressed me in a party dress, and then had me wait in the living room.

A man servant came to report to Mother that a *becak* (pronounced as bai-chak: a pedal-operated tricycle) had been ordered and a round trip fee to the library was negotiated. The evenings were usually cool and breezy. Riding in a becak under a clear starry night sky stimulated one to dream. Best of all, Mother was relaxed and enjoyed my companionship. I deeply wished there were more 'special occasions' like these library becak trips with Mother.

Every week she borrowed a high stack of Dutch novels, romance, history books, and fairy tales. She wished her life was different, and in her fantasies she traveled all over Europe. Names for her three daughters were found in these books. These library visits introduced me to a world of fairy tales, which Mother read me at bedtime. These tales eased me into sleep and inspired me to dream the impossible. 'One Thousand and One Nights' let me experience flying on a mat. 'Hansel and Gretel' in which Gretel intuitively saved herself and her brother, Hans, by tricking the wicked witch into the oven fascinated me.

Like Grandma, Mother strongly believed that only sons offered their mothers a bright and secured future as she aged. Mother had wanted a son with all of her heart. If only she had a son her life would be different. She would not be shunned by society and would have the promise of a financially secured future. So she believed.

Her first-born was Valerie, my sister. On her first birthday, April 11, 1931, Valerie was given to Grandma. Three months later I was born. Another girl? How disappointed she was! Mother was further away from achieving her life dream. When three years later my younger sister, Maud, was born, Mother was totally devastated. Endowed with three daughters but no sons, and a husband who was not interested in gathering wealth, Mother felt threatened.

I did not quite understand her frightening future without a son. I was confused and thought that there was something wrong by being a girl because it saddened Mother so deeply. I longed to prove her wrong.

At the age of five, I contracted a poliovirus, which left me with a crippled left hand. When it came to a handicap, Mother influenced by medieval ideas and beliefs believed that it was a punishment from God. So did society at large at that time. My physical disability added to her disappointment and misery in life. She focused on working harder and harder for the sake of reaching a better and secure future.

I got along very well with boys without having the desire to be a boy or dress like them. I was eager to compete with them in math and other subjects. I only shied away from sports, not knowing what to do with my left hand. I was always delighted to win any race, and found pleasure in more and greater academic achievements. By concentrating on being a very competitive student, I neglected my feminine qualities like to raise questions, such as: "Do you see me?" "Can you listen to me?" "Do you care whether you see me or not?" I cared deeply for my feminine looks! I mourned my physical disability and developed great regret for everything I could not do. For years I did just that—regret and mourn. Simultaneously, I felt a deep yearning for something I could not identify.

My father, Tan Thiam Sing, on the other hand was quite different than Mother. He was the one who gave me the feeling of: 'Gosh, I am somebody' or 'He is happy that I am here.'

Father at age 61

The family of my father settled in Ambarawa, a small town in central Java. They also came to Indonesia to find better lives through trading, but remained loyal to Confucianism and held high the Chinese traditions. Like most of that time, my parents' marriage was arranged. It happened that my father's cousin had married my mother's cousin a couple of years earlier. Word got around that the families were mutually compatible so my father's parents arranged a visit to my mother's parents with the sole purpose of meeting my mother. They were delighted with her, a follow-up visit was arranged, and they asked her hand in marriage on behalf of their son. Finally, the potential bride and groom met.

Mother's parents consulted their brothers and sisters for approval. Mother liked Father, and there were no objections from the relatives. Her parents invited Father's parents for a return visit and the proposal was accepted. The wedding was an extravagant celebration with a *gamelan* (Indonesian musical ensemble) to which the whole community was invited.

On July 19, 1931, I was born at Regentslaan 23—my maternal grandma's house in Salatiga—and named Tan Kwie Hwa. Mother gave me a Dutch name too, Constance, and called me Connie. After my birth, my parents and

I lived in Semarang, the capital city of the province of Central Java, on the island of Java.

Father was a retailer of imported fine foods and freshly baked goods. Mother operated the bakery and catering business. The family occupied two buildings next door to each other. One was arranged as a living room, a guest room, my bedroom, a study, and the nanny's corner. The other contained the shop, my parents' bedroom, an office, and a dining room. A corridor linked that front part of the first building to an open-air kitchen. Behind the kitchen a door opened into the bakery with a back door opening to the side street.

Our household had a nanny/housekeeper, a wash maid, and a cook. The shop had an errand boy. The bakery employed three bakers and the catering business had one or two cooks, depending on the demand. Only the nanny lived with the family.

My first becak ride was with Father when becaks were first introduced to Semarang in 1937. Minah dressed me in my loveliest—periwinkle white flowered dress, and impressed upon me the special quality of this new experience. We enjoyed our first becak ride in the cool evening after a humid tropical day. Sweet fragrance of jasmine flowers filled the air as we rode through the nicest part of town, the area where the governor of Central Java resided. In order to get there, however, we had to ride past a smelly, dirty canal—the most unpleasant part of the ride. Although I noticed the difference between the beautiful and neglected areas of the city, I assumed that the differences were the way life was. As we gazed at the darkening blue sky with its abundant stars and fascinating constellations, the driver silently pedaled until we got to a boulevard lined with palm trees. We were lost in our own thoughts and dreams, unaware of a brewing war or the beginning of a life-threatening illness in Mother. Occasionally chirping crickets disturbed the silence. Father appreciated being present in the moment. He seemed not to be worried about anything in the world.

Father was a sensitive, understanding, and easygoing person. He managed the family shop of fine bakery and imported goods, but lacked the drive to run the business as Mother wanted. Sometimes he would allow a customer time to consider and reconsider a purchase. Mother would have liked him to have more initiative as a sales person but my father, unencumbered by ambition, had no interest in status, and was untouched by tomorrow's worries.

In Grandma's eyes he was an under-productive bread-winner. While Mother worked exceptionally hard with a view of reaching the next level of wealth and social status, Father did not see the merit for working hard without enjoying life. It was difficult for him to meet Mother's demands.

Father loved to play Chinese checkers and card games. His hobby was entertaining friends. I treasured the time we played games together. I inherited my love for games from him. Winning gave me a thrill and a sense of joy and satisfaction. We did not talk much while we played. If Mother passed by and heard me exclaim, "I won!" she would say: *"Er wordt hier alleen Hollands gesproken!"* (Dutch is the only spoken language in this household!) We continued with another game as if nothing important had happened. I felt safe, and secure. We understood each other, Father and I.

He spoke English and Chinese and had a good command of the Indonesian language. He refused to adopt the Dutch culture or Christianity, and remained faithful to his Chinese culture and the teachings of Confucius.

His loyalty was to the Kuo Min Tang government, which was co-founded by Sun Yat-Sen (1866–1925). Sun's chief legacy was a philosophy known as the "Three Principles of the People: Nationalism, Democracy, and Peoples' Livelihood." My father was a true Chinese patriot. "To thine own self be true," a line quoted from Shakespeare, was his motto.

One day, when I was seven, Father received a shipment

of the finest Dutch chocolate from an importer. He gave each of us a taste of the smooth, delicious chocolate, each morsel wrapped in attractive, shiny paper. The next day I found one piece in my lunch box. All my friends envied me that day. I wanted to give each a bite. I assumed that these chocolates were expensive and I was sure Father would not let me take a dozen to school. So I figured out how to get them anyway without his permission.

I deliberately woke up very early one morning, dressed for school, and silently tiptoed to the store. I dragged a stool to the jars of chocolates on the top shelf. I carefully climbed up the stool, and, as I reached for the lid of the jar, I heard Father's footsteps behind me. My heart began to beat very fast, I was perspiring, and my hands felt very cold. Father, still in his blue striped pajamas, softly asked, "Can I help you? What kind of chocolate would you like to have today? Why in the dark? We better put the light on, don't you think?" I shivered and unable to utter a word, climbed down and got off the stool. He calmed me down and waited until I could tell him that I wanted to give chocolates to my friends at school. Teary-eyed and trembling with fear, I listened while he explained that these chocolates were not there to be given away—they were for sale. "If you would have asked me I would have given you some," he said. "Don't ever do it again. This is stealing.

You are taking something that does not belong to you." He gave me half a dozen. I calmed down with a flood of relief and renewed happiness. My father lovingly taught me the painful lesson that boundaries had to be respected. I could not have everything I wanted even though I was the apple of his eye. Later, when I was tempted to take sweets to school to buy friendships, memory of that event brought me back to reality.

Mother fell seriously ill due to high blood pressure in May of 1940 at the age of 36. She took Maud with her to stay with Grandma who lived in Salatiga. During that time Aunt June, Father's younger sister, came to stay with us and took care of me. Somehow mBok Minah was not around anymore.

One morning as I was waking up, Aunt June came to my bed, put her arms around me and said with tears in her eyes: "Connie, God has called your mommy home. She is not sick anymore. She has gone to heaven." I did not understand what that actually meant. Unmoved by the news I continued getting ready for school. Aunt June said, "You aren't going to school today. Instead, we are going to say farewell to your mother." I do not recall exactly what my response was. Perhaps I did not understand what my mother's death meant. I was nine years old. Did it mean no more trips to the library? Her death left me feeling ambivalent. I wondered if she was unable to be a loving mother to me, since she had wanted a son. I wondered if there ever was a bond between us that I had not realized. I still treasured her bedtime stories and felt her presence as a loving mother. Our bedtime stories might have been an apology for her negligence in many other parts of my life. I have no recollection of the funeral. She was laid to rest on June 9, 1940, the day that was supposed to be the grand opening of 'Astoria,' the restaurant she had built.

After her death my sisters and I lived with Grandma Hwie Nio.

During and right after WWII, the two towns, Semarang, where Father lived, and Salatiga, where we lived, were politically separated. Geographically the towns were only 40 miles apart. The Dutch-occupied Salatiga and Semarang was yet-to-be proclaimed Indonesia. Although we did not see much of each other, the bonds between my father and his three daughters were never broken. After President Sukarno proclaimed Indonesia's Independence from the Dutch, the two isolated areas were reunited.

After that, Father came more regularly to see Grandma and the family. I always looked forward to those weekends. On Saturdays, Grandma made sure there were fresh white and pink rose petals in the house. We gathered them into cotton flour bags, ready to take to Mother's grave the next morning. On Sunday mornings after church, Father, Valerie, Maud, and I took an *andong* (horse cart) ride to the cemetery where Mother was laid to rest. We scattered the rose petals on her grave, Grandpa's grave, and others. This was how we honored our dead ancestors.

With Mother's early passing, separated from my father, and raised by my maternal grandmother, I often felt rejected, abandoned, and isolated. The best place to go was to the small courtyard at the center of Grandma's house where I sat on the tiled floor, gazed up, and longed to see a falling star.

Chapter Three

Grandma was deeply concerned with my handicap. She was the one who arranged for me to get massage therapy in Surakarta, 35 miles southeast of Salatiga. Three times a week a masseuse came in a fancy carriage drawn by two horses to grandma's sister's house where I stayed for two weeks at a time. Her visits attracted the neighbor's attention as it was a big affair and honor to have a masseuse from the Sultan's palace come to visit an ordinary resident. Preparing for the arrival of the masseuse generated great excitement for everybody in the house. One maid boiled water, gathered the pot and towels, and placed them on a low wooden table, while another made sure the massage room and the living room were set up properly. On these special days, grandma's sister dressed for a high-ranking visitor. Between sessions I was to soak my left hand in hot herbal water for ten minutes daily.

To attend Dr. Osborn's healing crusade in Batavia, the Dutch East Indies' capital that later became Jakarta—capital of Indonesia—was one of the train rides with Grandma I treasured. Perhaps it was just another way to get full attention from an adult. Like any other eight-year-olds I was happy to miss school for a week. I looked out of the window watching rice fields after rice fields. Imagining how grateful people were when after several months of patienltly waiting, harvest time finally arrived.

Grandma explored every single possibility of cure available for my handicap. When she heard of surgery as an option, she immediately looked into that possibility. Later, in 1965 when I was in Australia I consulted an orthopedic specialist who explained that my hand had reached the best stage of recovery possible from polio. I was satisfied and grateful. Grandma always made sure that I learned to live with my disability. In embroidery, for example, she would say: "When you could not bring the thread to the needle, than see whether you couldn't bring the needle to the thread." "Do not focus on what you couldn't do but on what you could do despite your handicap." How exciting it was—after trial and error—to experience the thrill of pulling a thread through a needle my unique way! Years later I realized that what mattered was not the deformity itself but how I related to it.

What often puzzled me was why Grandma as an independent woman, a respected lay leader and initiator at her church did not allow her daughters to be more educated, find their own vocation and explore the world.

She took charge of her own life, as well as the lives of her children and grandchildren. Grandma wanted everyone around her to follow her will and directions. She acted as if she was the only one who knew best. Grandma did this in the name of love, but her love turned into domination and power. I grew up to dislike her. In fact, I was scared of her, and vowed not to be like her, yet sometimes found myself acting the contrary. I tried to be discreet in my rebellion against her strict, strong will and ideas of what I should become. As determined as she was to send her son to medical school, so was I determined to become a teacher, instead of a baker or a housewife. I wanted something different.

Admittedly, though, her strong will and ability to control enabled her to help her son be successful, which solidified his ability to help her financially in bringing up the three orphans his sister left behind. Uncle Tiong and his family took us into their home in Semarang during our high school years. He financed the largest part of our schooling and wedding expenses for Maud and I. Uncle Tiong was a stern, strict, and distant man. Apparently he wanted to be an authority figure that believed in his own mind and will. This was how he protected himself from giving in to those whom he allowed a finger and reached for his hand.

Among his close friends, however, he was an amiable,

warm, and fun loving man. Years later, at my wedding in Brussels, Belgium, he gave me away with dignity and pride. He mellowed in his later years and allowed himself to show his affection and concern for my well-being.

Grandma also made sure her other daughter, Ellie, helped her carry the burden of daily caring for the three of us. She understood and accepted her life tasks, and that the only way to achieve them was with an iron fist. Her faith and disciplined life were solid. She became an invincible woman with great self-respect. Grandma embodied the father figure that I needed in my early years. Her focused, goal-oriented approach to life became my model for goal achievement. Her unwavering hope in difficult times guided me to stick it out when things became tough.

When the Indonesian War of Independence was over in 1949, things began to return to normal. Gradually and without fear people gained more confidence in the new government. Just like the new republic, my generation was eager to put our new vision to work. As if we were running out of time, we wanted to finish school as soon as possible. We could not afford to have graduations, celebrations, or vacations. There was no time to celebrate our achievements, and boasting over one's accomplishments was unchristian, Grandma would say.

Valerie, who lived with Grandma back in Salatiga,

got certified in fashion design and dressmaking. She also helped in the bakery and shop part of the time. With high school now behind me, Grandma and I fought about my future plans for education. I wanted to become a teacher. Grandma wished me to become a housewife. It was common for women to be obedient and subversively manipulate her husband and others around her. I rebelled. Mother's ungrounded fear: "a handicapped girl will never catch a rich husband," haunted me too. Her strong conviction of that fear motivated me to prove her otherwise. I was determined to show her that a daughter could do what she thought only a son could do. Career building became my priority and my gender or defected left hand was not going to be an obstacle for achieving that goal.

Considering I had a mind of my own, stubborn and independent, Grandma feared I ruined my chances to catch a Chinese-Indonesian husband. Grandma persuaded herself to believe that Uncle Tiong was the one who might have the greatest influence on me. She really thought if there was one who could handle and persuade me to become a more socially acceptable and submissive woman, it must be Uncle Tiong. But fortunately for me, he left me alone with my struggle.

Aunt Ellie who had let any chance of gaining a higher education go by, put her word in for me. She recalled the sacrifice she had made when Grandma did not allow her to study further than high school because she had to help Grandma earn enough to put her brother through medical school. She wanted to prevent me from enduring the pain of a life long regret. So she fully supported and encouraged me to pursue my dream of becoming a teacher.

My decision was firm. I wanted to go to a teacher's college in Surakarta. Grandma threatened to abandon me if I did not obey her. I countered her threat with a plan to pay for my own schooling by taking on odd jobs while attending school. I was determined to become independent and stand on my own two feet. Despite her threats, I registered at the teacher's college in Surakarta and was accepted. I found room and board at a minister's home.

The day came to leave. I said goodbye to Grandma. With big tears rolling over her cheeks, she handed me an envelope with my first month school and boarding fee, and allowance. Afraid that she might change her mind, I took it from her, and quickly ran to Aunt Ellie, who was waiting for me in a rented car, ready to leave. On the same night I wrote Grandma a letter thanking her for her love and care for me and told her that I loved her very much, and promised to write her about my new experience regularly.

Soon after settling in, I began to look for job possibilities. In those days a part-time day job was hard to find. They all wanted to hire people to work from nine to five. The teacher's college operated temporarily from two to eight in the evening, since they did not have their own building. Finding work seemed not to be an option. Grandma could have taken advantage of my predicament, confronted me with an I-told-you-so attitude, and insisted on my coming home. But she did not. Long before the end of the month she sent money and I never had to make late payments for anything. I thanked Grandma and Aunt Ellie for supporting me in this great opportunity. Above all I was deeply grateful that I could express my gratitude to Aunt Ellie many times while she was still alive.

Two years later, proudly with my teacher's college's diploma in my briefcase, I left Surakarta. In those days there were no grand graduations. Schools were more concerned with delivering graduates to their new jobs. I took the bus home to Grandma. A secret admirer slipped in a beautifully written proposal of marriage in my hand just as the bus started to leave. It came as a nuisance to me and coldly I turned it down. I wrote to tell him that I was determined to start my first job at a Christian primary school in Salatiga as soon as possible and wished him well. There was no time for a romance.

I was thrilled when I learned that I could get an interview with the principal two days after I arrived at Grandma's house. Grandma was happy I had taken a job and lived with her again. The following week I was a fifth grade teacher at a Christian School. From everywhere I sensed a swelling of eagerness to start anew. There was a strong drive to make up for times lost brought about by the war. A new spirit to build the country filled the air.

I wished Mother was around.

Chapter Four

I am a fifth grade teacher. Some of the students were older than the average fifth graders. I was not much older than some of them. Fortunately the age difference was not much of a problem for them in accepting my authority as their teacher. Perhaps the students were cooperative because they were eager to finish school and motivated to pursue their dreams as soon as possible. I enjoyed teaching and was confident that I was on the right track to self-sufficiency.

Although Grandma did not wholeheartedly agree with me about the value of the work that I had started, she could not deny that teaching, like any other work, was a fate of humankind. I think she would have agreed with Dean Koontz who mentioned in *A Big Little Life* that, if done with diligence and integrity, work is obedience to divine order, a form of repentance. The only thing Grandma regretted was that my job did not pay much.

About two years later, the president of the board came up with a new job proposal: to start a high school. I did not know what to say to that offer. I was flattered and scared. He was convinced that it was time to open a high school and I was the one who had to start it. There was no other choice for me than to accept this new position. Since a promotion in a teacher's world was seldom matched by increased financial rewards, this assignment did not come with higher pay.

It was quite an undertaking. We started the first class on the front verandah of a church member's house. I was the one and only full time salaried teacher. Four part-time teachers and I made up the whole teaching team. Aesthetically it was not an attractive place to work, but the spirit of building something new together was powerful and fun. Three years later, I was happy and honored we did it. With the exception of one, all the students passed the public school exam with high marks that year. The experience of having founded a school from scratch was rewarding and gave me deep satisfaction.

Forty-five years later, Ridwan Gunawan, whose father was president of the school board when we started, granted me a return trip to Indonesia to celebrate the school's 45th anniversary. I was overwhelmed and honored by his gesture of generosity. He and his wife, June, were graduates of that school. On Christmas 2000 about 100 graduates and ex-teachers were gathered in the church hall to celebrate our history as recipients of an initiative taken by Rev. Gunawan.

During my teaching years I took weekend classes in pedagogy for two years. Life at that time was very huried. Everyone wanted to catch up with the world's pace of development. With this diploma, I got a part-time job as an assistant professor in pedagogy at the Christian University that later became Satya Wacana University. I was one of the first BA graduates of the Educational Psychology faculty. With my new degree I left Grandma and the family for a teaching job in Jakarta and enrolled at the University of Indonesia to pursue my master's degree in pedagogy. My thesis, entitled *An Orphanage as a Substitute of Parenthood*, led me to a job as superintendent of Dorcas Orphanage.

The poorly handled transfer of leadership from the old to the new did not make the transition easy. My first three months at Dorcas were hell. On the first day, when the new leadership team took over, there was not even enough food for us to share our first meal. The laundry had piled up and there were no clean clothes to wear. Early in the evening, as the younger children were preparing for bed, all the lights in the whole building went off. One started to cry and scream and was soon joined by the rest. We found out later that Mateo the oldest boy, encouraged by several girls, had pulled the main fuse. My level of insecurity began to mount. I was met with suspicion and resistance. Did the children sense that I unconsciously reached out to them as an effort to seek solace and healing for my own wounds? Was I perhaps unable to let them feel that I was there for them? Met with anger, distrust, and frustration, I became aggressive. Fortunately no one got hurt or things broken. I was exhausted. The following months were still challenging but gradually change began to happen. I made it through and worked there for two years.

Approaching my 30th birthday I became depressed and sought psychological counsel. Reflecting on that period, I regret that the counseling community was not using deep imagination, the roots of which sustained our ancestors and simultaneously generated ideas for the future. I fully agree with Michael Meade who believes that if life becomes more attuned to the promptings and yearnings of the inner life, culture may become less random and accidental. Life becomes more purposeful and meaningful, less filled with fear and more imbued with beauty.

To my great surprise I became the first Winnifred Kiek scholar to study foster care at the University of Sydney and adoption at the University of Melbourne. That would be my first overseas trip. I was very excited and felt challenged. I wondered if I was living my mother's dream or mine? Maybe it was both hers and mine.

In Sydney I had to address an audience of church women one afternoon. Overwhelmed and deeply touched by their attention and warmth, I started to weep on the stage and was not able to continue my presentation about care for the orphan. I was not able to meet and accept my inner orphan yet and was unable to receive the intensity of care they bestowed on me and was deeply embarrassed.

One of my assignments was working at an 'Unwed Mothers' Home.' At that time the care for unwed mothers was a new and sensitive field. We could not openly talk about it. A small group of young pregnant girls between 13 – 16 years of age lived temporarily in the home. Considerable time was spent to help the girls participate in making the decision about their own and unborn child's future. In the adoption practice the acceptance of the unborn baby by its biological mother as well as its adoptive parents was considered of high value and critical to the well-being of the fetus. I was deeply touched.

At about the same time the *Gereformeerde Kerken* (Reform Church) in the Netherlands also offered me a scholarship to study about the operations of children's homes and a master's degree in pedagogy/psychology at the Vrije Universiteit (Free University) in Amsterdam. Both scholarships were offered in 1965 during the Coup d' Etat in Indonesia. I said farewell to Australia, and sailed off on an Italian/Australian cruise on December 6, 1965. In January 1966 I landed in Genoa, Italy, and took the train north to Baarn, the Netherlands.

As one of my practicum assignments I visited a School Social Work Center in Amsterdam. For two weeks I worked with Truuske Nortier to learn what service it provided to the teachers, parents, and students. In brief, School Social Work was an effort to help the teacher and parents to understand and guide a child with learning problems. I was impressed by how much time, energy, and money was spent to the individual child. I couldn't help but compare that service to the educational services in Indonesia at the time. It was an excellent service that not all schools could afford to provide. Most of all I was captured by Truuske's compassion for the socio-economically, culturally, physically, mentally challenged child.

Truuske—now in her early nineties—grew up in Malang, East Java, Indonesia. Her father was a physician at a missionary hospital in Malang. Shortly before WWII she and her twin sister, Suuske (deceased), returned to the Netherlands to continue further schooling.

Since my placement at the School Social Work Center, Truuske and I became friends. She invited me to a Sinterklaas (Santa Claus) celebration at her parents' house that year. Each one of us was given a task to find our individual gifts that were carefully hidden throughout the house. Presenting and performing the gift to the group was challenging and hilarious. It was a fun evening.

On our wedding day she surprised me with a red hibiscus plant.

She and Suuske visited our Kelapa Dua Community Development project in Indonesia while I was living in Belgium. Truuske introduced Adrie—her physician niece—to Kelapa Dua where two years later Adrie spent several years as a freelance physician.

In Amsterdam Truuske served on the ICA Board for several years. (More about ICA in Chapter Five). She painted, and was interested in craft. Occasionally she helped a minister for international students studying in the Netherlands collecting used furniture. We enjoyed van Gogh's paintings as much as the gamelan. Since now we both no longer travel long distances we treasure our Skype conversations very much.

Another woman in the Netherlands who had impacted my life was Rens van Netten. It was so good to reunite with her. Rens and I met in Indonesia where she worked as a theologian in a Javanese Protestant congregation in Central Java. She was studying clinical psychology at the University of Amsterdam. Our mutual interest was a flute and a *Rijsttafel* (Indonesian rice meal).

Rens loved to play the flute. During our walks in the woods of Indonesia and in the Netherlands we always found an interesting spot at a creek or under a shady tree. We stopped. She took her wooden flute out of her backpack and played a tune and I sang. I was also attracted by a flute, but could not play it. Deeply I regretted.

Living on a student budget could be challenging sometimes. But we managed to treat ourselves at very special occasions—after her graduation— on a Rijsttafel. We met at The Hague Central Station and took a tram to a luxurious restaurant where we stayed for the day to enjoy a conversation and a fine meal. A *Rijsttafel* consisted of a rice bowl presented on an elegant tray and surrounded by 24 dainty and delightful dishes. There were chicken and pork satay, stewed beef in a coconut sauce, spicy roasted shredded coconut with peanuts, vegetables in coconut sauce, and shrimp chips among others.

Until about five years before her death in 2012 Rens was occupied with the oppression of the feminine soul in both women and men. She learned about the oppression of women in countries such as Afghanistan, India, and Rwanda from friends who worked in those countries as missionaries. She also spoke about her own painful experience in Indonesia, where as a woman theologian she was not allowed to deliver the gospel from the pulpit or serve the sacraments while her Dutch and Indonesian men colleagues could.

I had my diploma and visited orphanages in search for more and better solutions for the orphans in Indonesia, while I hungered for a connection to home I still had to find. Offering me the scholarships might have disappointed the Australian Church Women and the Reformed Churches in the Netherlands for leaving the field in search of that connection. I regretted I did not meet their expectations.

Upon return to Indonesia I took a job as a childcare coordinator. I channeled funds to orphanages and provided training to orphanage staff across Indonesia. More and greater achievements and travel opportunities came up. I was beginning to satisfy Mother's wish for success and achievement as a girl with a crippled left hand! I still did not heed the yearnings of my soul.

I often wondered where all my meanderings from orphanage to orphanage were leading me. Gradually I became aware that reaching out to my inner orphan was most crucial in healing my wounds of abandonment. At the same time it was also crucial to develop my capacities to adequately carry out my job. How is success or failure of a scholarship awarded to a yearning soul measured?

Chapter Five

On the way to friends in Sun City Festival, Arizona, in 2007 we crossed a development where large pieces of land were being tilled. There were a few new houses and more were under construction. A lady neighbor of our friends was digging and loosening the soil in front of her house. Sweat dripped from her face. Gravel, dirt, and sand flew in different directions. "I want geraniums, snap dragons, and petunias here under the window," she explained as we stopped to chat. "Wouldn't it be gorgeous? But there's so much work to be done before I get that far. Loosening up the soil is the hardest and most important part of the project," she said to encourage herself.

She reminded me of the time I first worked on loosening my fixed, rigid attitudes and beliefs. My mother's nightmare: "A handicapped girl will never catch a rich husband," had also become mine. That fear stayed with me for a long, long time. I tried to suppress it, but at odd times it surfaced until it got my attention.

In 1970, when I was in my late thirties, I came across a strange and fascinating movement, which had a variety of names, the Ecumenical Institute (EI), The Institute of Cultural Affairs (ICA), and the Order Ecumenical (OE). This movement, and my involvement in it, plays a role in the next several chapters. For convenience, I will refer to it as the Institute of Cultural Affairs or the ICA. The ICA was a not-for-profit organization founded by Dr. Joseph W. Mathews, his wife Lyn, three other ministers, and their wives.

Joseph Mathews, known as Joe, was the initiator. Joe became the Dean of the ICA-USA, a post he held until his death in 1977. I met Joe in Indonesia through a weekend course entitled Religious Studies-One (RS-One) that he and his team designed and offered in the US and in other parts of the world. RS-One was designed to awaken church members to the task of becoming conscious of themselves and their vocation as people who care for all of humanity in the contemporary world. The organization carried out this task by creating structural care systems.

I was deeply impressed by a section of the course that focused on understanding Jesus the Christ in a 20th century context, which was called the Christ Lecture. It helped me to understand how to fully live my life as a woman with a deformed hand. "Your past is approved, your present received, and your future open: all is possible," was a line in the Christ Lecture that held me captive for quite some time. That sudden awareness felt like what the neuro-scientist would call an evolutionary jump. To affirm that all is possible implied that I did not have to prove myself. I did not have to earn affirmation. I learned that anyone could attain this state of mind when one says 'yes' to all of life. To live my life from this new understanding was quite a different matter. It did not just happen. I had to struggle to make it happen.

The late Brian Stanfield, an Australian ICA colleague, once said: "When we step into the waters of life, and see the waves running high, it is difficult to remember the openness of the future." How did "... your future is open" apply in my situation? Did it mean it was OK for me to be a woman with a deformity? Could I achieve my dreams, get married, and travel the world? That was not what Mother taught me to believe. I began to negate the imposed convictions that haunted me. Addressed by these words of possibility, I began to wonder how these ideas applied in my life from that point forward. I was scared.

I was at the height of my career as a private sector childcare coordinator for orphanages and community centers across Indonesia. I designed and conducted staff in-service-training programs and attended international conferences. I loved my work, travels and meeting people from different countries and cultures. I hired a young girl, who cooked, did laundry, and other chores. Mother would have been very proud of me. I wished she had been around to witness it. But I was also at the brink of an emotional breakdown. I was bossing others around, including my boss. Though surrounded by people, I felt isolated and excluded. The longing for an intimacy and deeper connection caused much anxiety. Although I had many business relationships, for instance the office staff, community workers, and board members of orphanages, yet a connection with anyone of them, or with myself was missing. Frustrated, I lashed out at my boss. I lost my job.

In 1973 ICA International was recruiting for international expansion. Strongly attracted to participate in social change, I impulsively became a member of ICA's international staff. At that time ICA was organized as a community that offered its members room, board, and a small stipend. It provided security and a wide range of participation and training possibilities. ICA did not employ people to develop community; instead it invited people to participate in reformulating their own community.

I did not allow myself to fully experience my depression, and accept the imbalance of my soul. Instead I ran away from my reality and hid behind the pretense of serving others and promoting social change. I was longing for acceptance, but I acted as if others around me were the ones who needed to accept themselves. I refused to feel the pain of disconnection and the ache of loneliness.

What impressed me most about Joe was his deep passion for authentic human living, which, he believed, was a birthright for all. He was trying to embody the lived meaning of the existential impact of a rational concept of faith. He saw his life's task to be a quest to find clarifying concepts of faith in life experiences of the individual in relationship to her/his community. Total life expenditure meant living one's life fully. Joe's vision was to create a community of care and he needed people to participate in building that community. Not only did he have the ability to convince people to see his vision, join in, and actively participate to reach that goal, but also most strikingly he gave himself totally to the effort. Although his dedication and commitment to his goal helped me to identify my own calling, I questioned his style of achieving that goal.

My first assignment was as part of the Institute's staff in Indonesia. The ICA had initiated Fifth City, a community reformulation project in Chicago. As a pilot project, Fifth City yielded insights and wisdom that could be applied in other locations. In 1976, Kelapa Dua, Indonesia, was chosen to be one of 24 replication projects around the globe. Joe pushed for a replication project in Indonesia to show what could be done worldwide. I felt pressured to initiate a community reformulation project while the people of Kelapa Dua were not ready to participate in taking up responsibility for their own community. The majority of the people was still living in their traditional worldview and did not foster the desire to think for themselves. They were more inclined to follow a leader than participate in reaching a group consensus.

On the day we were supposed to see the officials for approval to hold a public meeting, I locked myself up in my room. I was scared and feared the risk I was taking. The international staff was ready, but not the villagers. Neither was I. My opinion was disregarded, and Joe's urgency to complete his project got priority. Reluctantly, at the last minute, I gave in to his idea. We got permission to hold a week long planning session with the villagers, the local authorities, and the ICA International staff which resulted in a community reformulation project in Indonesia one of 24 replication projects across the globe. That was Joe's dream, not mine. Although I deeply resented being pressured, I went along with the group's decisions, fearing loss of admiration and acceptance.

We wanted to have the villagers participate in transforming a muddy trail into a graveled road to make transporting their crop to the adjacent town for sale, easier. It was our hope that this project became a showcase of a participative community effort. People came to the planning session, got excited about having a graveled road, but when it came down to the work, people shrank from the responsibility it required. They were scared and lost courage to continue to work on the project. They were not used to achieve anything they wanted to have. To build a road together was an unimaginable undertaking. One man signed up for a trip to a gravel store to ask for donated gravel and others promised to be at the site at the set time and place. None of them showed up! The ICA staff - excluding me - graveled the muddy road, while the people who were invited to participate, just watched. They did not believe it was going to happen because they never had seen a dream come into realization. It was an arduous, painful effort, both transforming the muddy road and observing my unchanged and hardened beliefs. I realized that I had been arrogant and now felt humiliated. I was used to having others working for me. Since I was born I had people around me whom I thought were born to serve: that was what I was taught to believe. Bad attitudes die hard, people say. Hardened soil had to be loosened up before new seeds could be planted.

Three years later, after Joe's death, I understood that life had been fleeting for him and he did not want to waste precious time on unrelated matters such as personal growth and transformation, which he labeled navel-gazing. In his opinion there was no time to wait until people were ready to participate in achieving a goal. He had to go ahead in realizing his dream.

During the early years with ICA, I participated in an experiment of consensus building. Blindly I accepted the stance, rules, and directions handed down by the leaders. There was no difference in the way I accepted and trusted guidelines of my previous belief system. Only the content was different. We did not see the importance of inner connection to our individual core or psyche, which I learned was vital to the discovery of our own calling. The connection allows us to find that certain something into which we pour our passion. As Joe was able to lead a full, rich, and happy life, so each one of us could. I had to find mine.

Being part of his global team was a time to shed my worn-out belief systems. I used to believe that God, the church, and our parents decided our destiny. I would be punished for my disobedience to whatever had been decided for me. I was not allowed to change, but had just to accept my situation. As part of Joe's team, I experienced another way of looking at life: everyone could make a change. In Kelapa Dua I did things I never had done before, such as going from door-to-door to invite people to a workday or decide on behalf of those who were not ready to make their dream come true.

My next global assignment was to ICA-Amsterdam, which did not come as a surprise to me. Constant change was what one could expect from being an ICA member. We were not out to create establishments, but to enable communities and individuals to create their own, to change, and to grow. As much as I dreaded change, I loved to travel, especially to be in Europe again.

In the fall of 1977, I arrived at Schiphol, the Netherlands. The office was located at Rosengracht (Rose Canal), in Amsterdam. In the seventeenth century, Amsterdam became one of the most important trade ports in the world as a result of its innovative trade practices and monopoly in Asia. The city was, and still is, the financial and cultural capital of the Netherlands. I could not help but think how much Mother would have appreciated being there with me as I began my international assignment. As part of the ICA-Amsterdam staff, I helped introduce its consensus building methodology through a program of community meetings, called Dorpsdag (community day). My role was to be a global presence in our small ICA community. A British man, a Dutch woman, four Americans, and I, an Indonesian, made up the staff. Two of us had to earn our daily living by taking jobs, one or two worked at the office, and the rest traveled to promote or teach the consensus building process.

Office work and promoting the courses we offered was my primary work. How much I wished to teach the courses. English was the medium for teaching. Part of the course was taught in Dutch and must be taught by Dutch native speakers. I was not comfortable to teach the course in consensus building in either English or Dutch. I was frustrated. In order to keep up my spirit, regularly I was called to help our European head office, located in Brussels, with fundraising for our community reformulation projects in Africa and India.

After having had two adventurous years at the Kelapa Dua community reformulation project and as an educated Indonesian woman of Chinese descent in Amsterdam, I found myself a third world presence in a former colonial master's world. No matter how international we would have liked to be in Indonesia or in the Netherlands, ICA was an American initiative, whose influential power had always to be considered. To please leaders was still my undesired tendency. To stand up for myself was what I could not do. Blaming leaders for not allowing me to teach, for instance, was easier to do than suggesting a plan to master the spoken language that enabled me to teach.

I was angry at myself for my inability to express what I thought or felt.

By bringing up this memory of my struggle with the past a possibility began to present itself as if I could become the mother I had wanted. I felt like tilling the soil to make a beautiful, strong 'something' grow. I became my mother wanting out, and me—her daughter—who could find a way to make it happen.

Chapter Six

In the spring of 1979 I had cataract surgery in Amsterdam. Anticipating a new ICA assignment, I moved to Brussels to recover. I moved into a large room with a high ceiling and a large window on the second floor over looking a small garden. Every year, between the last week of August and mid September, ICA conducted a Tribal Resettlement, which involved moves of both living and working spaces. I did not anticipate staying in that room for long.

Every other year in August there is an enormous "flower carpet" display at Grand Place in the heart of the city of Brussels. Thousands of colorful begonias are arranged in patterns that cover a total area of about 18,000 square feet. This display of flowers attracts many tourists from all over the world since it was introduced in 1971. It reminded me of a much larger flower display, the Keukenhof (kitchen garden), and known as the Garden of Europe, in Lisse, South Holland, the Netherlands.

August was a month of change for our ICA community: for some it was a coming back from a summer break. For others, like me, it meant taking up a new assignment at a new place. It was a new year with different plans and challenges, and different work and living spaces. We moved from an old to a new location physically, psychologically, culturally, and socially. Since 1979 was the year of the flower carpet, we all agreed to celebrate our move with a visit to the flower carpet at Grand Place. It was a big thrill!

The periodic moves challenged us to reorient ourselves to where we were on our journey as a community and as individuals. We learned to detach ourselves from possessions, places, and people. Each move provided an opportunity to employ our creativity and expand our inventive capacities. A change of staff meant having new people with fresh perspectives to view a too familiar situation.

The annual changes of staff encouraged us to cross thresholds and move into new, unexplored territories of caring for ourselves, others, and the environment. Being constantly on the move affected me in various ways. They were reminders of my past, when at Grandma's or Uncle Tiong's households I had felt I did not belong, and was drawn to seek and create my own home. I always had the feeling of being a visitor on the way to some place else. Now, as I reflect on those frequent moves, I appreciate having developed the ability to create a temporary connection to a place and still be able to call it home.

We began our ICA style relocation process with a meeting to set the context for the move. Recommendations for new rooms were posted on a bulletin board for everyone's approval. Changes were considered and accepted before the move. Some of us enthusiastically began to pack, move, and organize the newly assigned room. Others discussed it with their spouses and close friends. Always attached to the old and familiar, I needed time to part with it and found it extremely hard to welcome change. I loved to look at my small treasures collected from places I had been, such as Saraswati, the Hindu Goddess of Art and Science, from one of my trips to Bali with my nephew, Hauw (pronounced as how), Valerie's only son. Another statue was of another Hindu Goddess Kali, Protector and Destroyer, from a visit to Bombay (Mumbai) where I taught a Women's Forum. Instead of packing, I lingered on the memories. A small oil painting I bought in Vienna, Austria, reminded me of the time I wandered around in Stephanplatz after a business visit to the provincial office of the Benedictines who supported our work in India and Africa. It was G. Millet's painting, L' Angelus, of a man and a woman on a field at sunset, saying a prayer of gratitude and praise after a hard day's work which years later Vincent van Gogh painted and named it The Evening Angelus. It reminded me of Grandma's daily prayer life.

I took time to recall the experiences associated with each item, which made me the last one to move out of my room. Taking my time always had kept someone else from moving into my vacated room on time. Although I hated moving, even if it was only from one room to another in the same building, somehow, I managed to make each move. Just the effort brought back all the previous memories of moves I had made.

I remembered the first summer holiday after Mother's death. During the whole summer break of 1940, I stayed with Valerie and Maud at Grandma's house. We had so much fun the four weeks we were together. Then came the time to say goodbye. Since Maud was only six years old, she was allowed to stay with Valerie at Grandma's house, but I had to go back to my father's house. Grandma took me back to my father's by bus. When it came time for her to leave, I cried and cried while holding tightly onto her beautiful blouse, and refused to let her go. She missed the bus. I clung to her blouse until both she and my father came up with an arrangement allowing me to live with her and my sisters.

I had ambivalent feelings about Grandma. On one hand I hated her and feared she might look down upon me as she did my father, and on the other hand, I admired her unwavering faith in life especially in times of great sorrow. The loss of the becak rides to the library with Mother was too hard to bear alone. I needed my sisters' company to help carry that burden. The following week I moved back to Grandma's home. That was my first move, at the age of nine.

The 1979 ICA move was celebrated with a trip to the flower carpet and a feast during which we reflected on the process of moving. We told stories of moving and what it did to us as a community, and as individuals. It was a good exercise to remind us of what we were about, and made us aware that at any moment we could create a new understanding, move to a new space, and relate to it in a new way. Moving inspired a sense of expansiveness. Periodic relocations created an awareness that life is larger than one's place, age, and achievements.

Louise DeSalvo, author of *On Moving* says that moving to a new place affords us the opportunity to make changes in our lives, but it is we who must make those changes. They don't happen automatically. As a member of a group that had learned to reflect, I found it very helpful to know about myself, to understand where I had been, and where and when I must go. Newly gained insight did not automatically initiate changes in my behavior. If real changes were to happen, I had to address deeply rooted attitudes, which stood in the way of personal growth and to let go of worn-out beliefs. Letting go did not come easy.

Meanwhile, my sister, Maud, had become seriously ill in Indonesia. I had not seen her, Valerie, or their families for over three years. Maud was in denial of her battle against ovarian cancer. She believed that suffering the pain that God had given her was a noble Christian act of faith. I found myself irritated and angry about her Christian beliefs related to her illness. Then I realized that there was no difference between her blind faith and obedience to her faith and my belief in a vision of a changed society, and my submission to the expectation of ICA. I longed to be with her in her final hours, but as a loyal member of the ICA community, I did not feel I had the right or muster up the courage to request time off. I seemed to have given up on being a person with choices. After all, it was easier to blame the community for not allowing me to make decisions. I was overly concerned with prestige and power. I had denigrated my heart and emotions. I denied the pain of loneliness. The wounds of loss sat unhealed in the depths of my soul. Years later in analysis I discovered how estranged I was from my feelings. The state of my psyche was like what Clarissa Pinkola Estes, in *Warming the Stone*

Child described as having many accomplishments, yet not feeling as if I had accomplished anything. She called that the psyche of an unmothered child. I felt captured, locked up, and not free at all. I wanted change, but did not dare to make that change.

So I designed a plan to reach my personal goal for change. I had learned that women were not supposed to express the aching hunger for a relationship with a man. My family did not arrange my marriage as had been done in previous generations. I also realized that Mother's voice had become mine: "A poor girl with a deformity will never catch a rich husband. Like me, you'll never travel nor see the world." It was neither the community nor my relatives who had prohibited me from carrying out my plan. It was I who did not give myself permission to initiate a relationship with a man. The clock was ticking—I was approaching fifty.

I decided to look for a husband in the ICA community. There were not many prospects to choose from and certainly no Indonesians. I still carried my mother's prejudice. I must have looked and acted desperate! Male colleagues— their wives more so—avoided my company. People poked fun at me for the evident uncontrollable emotions that I exuded widely. I scared my priest colleagues by being extra helpful to them in order to get their attention. My colleagues became puzzled about my focused dedication to the task of fundraising, and tried to figure out what was stoking the fire for my action. "Was she interested in seducing a priest who clearly was not even considering renouncing his vow?" I overheard an abrupt remark: "...at best to be a housekeeper in his presbytery?" The humiliation was excruciating.

We were a bunch of people at a cross road, questioning others and ourselves. Many of us were dealing with the question: "What is this golden thread that connects our souls to our real task that breathes divine fire and brings our work to life?" as author--Phil Cousineau--of *Stoking the Creative Fires* would ask.

The Thorn Birds, a novel by Colleen McCullough, was popular at that time. The story, which takes place on an Australian sheep farm, portrays the struggle of Father Ralph, a parish priest, with his growing awareness of two different relationships: one with Mary Carson, a wealthy, witty widow and the other little Meggie who, for some mysterious reason, mattered so much to him. I identified with Mary Carson, a woman who displayed deep-seated jealousy and possessiveness when it came to Father Ralph and other women. I partially identified with her attraction and relationship to him, excluding physical attractions and sexual escapades. I empathized with her isolation and loneliness, which I found to be unbearable and humiliating! The only way for me to work through my own isolation and loneliness was to develop my own experience. Frantically I refused to die a nun. That I did. For the first time in my life I mustered courage to disturb the comfort of familiar roles in order to discover the true face beneath family and cultural conditioning.

One day the group was attending an ICA annual district meeting in Poperinge, Belgium. During a lunch break some of us visited a nearby health food store. I noticed a man who was interested in the same food items as I, which led to a conversation about *Sambal*, an Indonesian chili sauce, my favorite condiment. All members of the ICA community were dressed in navy blue, but this man had a distinctive way of adding a matching tie or handkerchief to his attire. He was tall, handsome, and well dressed. Our conversation continued and I learned that he was with ICA-Amsterdam. His name was Tom. His last name, Reemtsma, sounded Dutch, but his paternal ancestors were Germans. Secretly I wished to get to know him better, and hoped that he spoke Dutch. I began to regret our community's revolutionary stance: to put our mission above our individual life's demands. This ideal did not allow us to see each other as often as I would have liked. At that time our community was challenging the individualistic life-style. We were supposed to be image-shifters and were expected to put our individual needs aside for the sake of the mission. Without realizing it, again I had suppressed an unfulfilled emotional instinct by pretending that I needed nothing relational.

Tom was ten years my junior. I thought about him more and more, wondering if he would be a good partner and wondering if he was even interested in me. Despite Mother's early warnings, my disabled hand did not seem to bother Tom. It became clear that both of us were tired of living the single life. We talked about our past. Tom revealed that some childhood wounds had made him determined to develop his own voice. He had embarked on a journey to find his unique self. That year, 1981, we went to England for a summer vacation and got to know each other better. At heart Tom was a real gentleman, always ready to please people, especially women. We entered a fondue restaurant one evening. Graciously he took my coat and held my chair, and assisted me to sit at the table. Suddenly and simultaneously, we said: "Oh, this is not the way we're supposed to act as social revolutionaries." Immediately I added: "I'm an emancipated woman. I can seat myself." "Yes, that's right. I don't have to do this. But I would like to do it anyway," he replied.

Tom loved to set tea the English way. Until then I only

knew how to set and drink tea the Indonesian and the ICA community ways. At Grandma's house we set tea in a large pot for the whole day. Every so often it got refilled with hot water. We had strong tea in the morning and weak tea by the end of the day. The ICA community tea setting was different in each location, depending on the people who made up the staff and where they were located. Tom liked to set tea precisely for five minutes. Indeed, Tom's style of tea setting tasted better.

I could not say that we were in love with each other then. We were intrigued and repelled by each other. We were attracted, scared, and irritated by each other. We loved each other's company. Yet we liked our privacy and solitude—to be in our own thoughts and world. Both of us wanted to be understood and allowed to live in our own worlds. During our ten days in Great Britain we enjoyed the train rides, museum visits, conversations, and, above all, having tea together. By the end of the trip we decided to request the ICA leadership to assign us to the same office and location. We were interested in finding out if living as a couple was indeed what we wanted.

In the fall of 1981 we were assigned as staff members to ICA-Brussels. We had so much fun exploring Brussels! The Portuguese and Italian festivals in our neighborhood were exquisite. We loved Belgian cuisine, especially the mussels and fries, and French crepes with bacon and cheese. Tom liked to cook and experiment with new recipes. On family nights I had the chance to taste his fabulous cooking. Frequently we explored favorite eateries. Then I discovered that Tom's paternal great grandfather was also a baker. Both of our families had ancestors who were bakers. When I heard that, a thrill passed through me. Our relationship was growing more intimate and tender.

The kitchen was a place we both seemed to appreciate and cherish. Somehow it provided familiarity, security, and warmth. One Wednesday afternoon Tom suggested we meet in the kitchen around midnight, for a light dessert he had bought. It was a very cold winter night. Every one had already gone to bed. Tom was dressed in his Sunday outfit and looked very handsome. As we were standing by the fireplace he nervously began to give a short speech about why we were there. He calmly and straightforwardly proposed to me. "Yes!" We celebrated with apple cobbler, Godiva chocolates, and a cup of hot chocolate. Then Tom suggested he call his parents right away, and announce our engagement to the community the following day.

Change requires constant learning and relearning. This teaching in the ICA community developed into regular meeting times and places which allowed us to converse and study in an atmosphere of cooperative ambience.

These meetings were held on Thursday evenings and called Ecclesiola or church-within-a-church. The Ecclesiola was elegantly designed to nourish body and soul. Despite my passive participation I was touched and nourished. It seemed that it was easier for me to talk about external and concrete events and ideas rather than about my feelings or relationships toward anything. Lacking proficiency of the English language was part of the problem, but mostly it was the disconnection deep within that held me back from participating on that level. The Ecclesiola was a live, active, and constantly creative ritual. There was always an aspect of newness to it, an aliveness that each participant took away. It was an event that nourished the soul.

On that particular Thursday evening, in the winter of 1982, we started an Ecclesiola with a typical Dutch meal. We were served Leidse kaas (cheese), crackers, and white wine as hors d'oeuvre. In the background *Op de Schone, Stille Heide* (On a Beautiful, Quiet Moorland), a Dutch song, was softly playing. The main dish was Dutch Erwten soep (pea soup) with sausage, rye bread and cheese. We finished the meal with custard. The group moved into what we originally called an Art Form Conversation that later became Focused Conversation. Brian Stanfield, in *The Art of Focused Conversation* mentioned that there is a trialogue between a piece of art, the artist, and the observer. It is through this trialogue that an experience is recreated and allows the observer to respond to the art object. That night the conversation was on Vincent van Gogh's Starry Night an oil painting that hung on the wall behind the head table. A centerpiece consisting of four different sizes of used paintbrushes were randomly set on a Delft-blue cloth on the center table. We all sat in a u-form seating arrangement with two facilitators sitting at the head table.

The conversation style we were about to use was formulated by Joe Mathews when as a chaplain in the US Army during WWII, he noticed how unequipped many of the soldiers were in facing situations that did not make any sense to them. Obsessed with the question of how to help people process their life experiences in search for meaning, he started his quest. He returned to his university professorship and was determined to develop the Focused Conversation Method, through which individuals find meaning for their personal and community life experiences. The intent of the study that evening was how to use the focused conversation method for conscious reflection to find and express one's values through mining the artist's values. A facilitator guided the group through the four levels of the process: the objective, the reflective, the interpretive and the decisional. On the objective level, he wanted us to make sure that we all were dealing with the same data. "What do you see?" "What colors do you notice?" The reflective level dealt with questions such as: "What does it remind you of?" "How does it make you feel?" On the interpretive level the facilitator asked: "What was it all about?" "What did it mean to you?" The last category of questions, the decisional level, was: "What do we say to the painting?" I was fascinated by the variety of answers from the participants, and I realized that I could participate without uttering my answers. At any level, if I wished to, I could express my feelings about a similar experience. Inhibited by my English, I kept answers to myself. Some identified the mood of van Gogh at the time he put the strokes on the canvas as longing for expansion of closely knitted communities. One participant noticed how burdened the village, including himself, was as a result of the teachings of his church. Another saw brightness in the midst of the darkness of inner suffering. One pointed out how hard it might have been for the artist to go against the grain in expressing who he was. On the final level of reflection, some responses were: "Continue the struggle to BE!" "Express that which calls to be expressed." I was in awe.

Then as the meeting was closing Tom stood up and announced our engagement to the group, handed me a bouquet of gorgeous red tulips, and gave me a warm kiss. It was the most memorable Ecclesiola ever!

In the spring of that year Tom and I were married. We both were fully aware that I was beyond childbearing age. The question we asked ourselves was, "What creativity would we both bring to this relationship that might become our legacy." We decided to compose a statement of our commitment to each other. Together we created a list of what a covenant and the task of a family needed to be. Out of the list we chose the ones that were most important to us. We wrote a statement and drew a symbol of our covenant. A description about the symbol is in Chapter Eight. This document was presented to the leadership at the congregational dinner the evening before the church wedding. My wedding dress, a gift from my stepmother, was gorgeous navy blue with pink, purple, and white flowers. I had chosen the ICA color blue for the dress so that I could wear it at other festive occasions. Surprisingly Tom ordered a fabulous bouquet of spring flowers in similar colors. Twenty-five years later I wore the dress again on our Silver Wedding Anniversary!

It was customary in Belgium that a civil wedding precedes the church wedding. Our civil wedding was held at the Saint Gilles City Hall Brussels. A week later we got married at *De Nederlandse Evangelische Hervormde*

Kerk (The Dutch Evangelic Reformed Church). When we returned for our 25th wedding anniversary we visited the church office and discovered that we had not signed the church registry book of weddings. We signed it then, 25 years later.

Tom had selected 13 ICA community songs to be sung before the bride entered the sanctuary. I wondered if he unconsciously wanted to delay the pronouncing of our vows. It was a long wait for me outside the church. Fortunately Rens van Netten, my dear Dutch friend as maid of honor, kept me company. When I entered the church, I saw about forty friends and relatives attending our fabulous spring wedding: Tom's parents had come from Davenport, Iowa, and his nephew, Andy Thorson, who was studying in Paris, were there. Uncle Tiong, his wife, daughter, son, and their respective families from the Netherlands were all present. A reception in the garden of the ICA community building followed with an exotic and delicious Indonesian luncheon catered and given by *Toko Jaya* (Indonesian Foods & Catering) in Amsterdam, owned by Tik & Khing, Uncle Tiong's son and daughter-in-law. Tom's parents—Mel and Marian Reemtsma-- presented us with around-the-world trip tickets for our honeymoon gift. The day after the wedding we left for London. We then made short visits to Bahrain and India, where we observed the sobering inconveniences of life. Bahrain, the first developing country Tom had visited, made a deep impression on him. In India, a German friend and ICA-India colleague, was our guide. He encouraged us to "go native" in the short time that we were there resulting in both of us experiencing diarrhea by the time we arrived in Thailand. Fortunately, we recovered and were able to enjoy Singapore and its legendary orderliness.

I was overjoyed to be met by Maud and Tjong, Aunt Ellie's son, and their families at the Sukarno-Hatta airport in Jakarta. Maud threw a fabulous party, a very warm welcome to us. It was a marvelous family affair and an opportunity for Tom to be introduced to my close relatives and friends. We stayed with Aunt Ellie at Grandma's family home, where I was born and lived after Mother died. We were thrilled to visit Valerie and her family in their home in Salatiga at the perfect time when the orchid garden was in full bloom, and the ripe, sweet mangoes were ready for picking. Maud and her family flew into town to complete the family gathering. It was as if we three sisters were in our own paradise where time was suspended and past, present, and future had come together just for us. We had a fabulous time, not realizing that this would be the last time we would be together.

I introduced Tom to *Candi* (pronounced as Chandi)

Borobudur, a spectacular Buddhist temple located southwest of Salatiga. This temple has been the center for pilgrimages and a popular tourists' attraction. 72 Buddha statues, seated inside a woven lattice fence, surround the main *stupa* (pronounced as stoo-pa: dome) located at the center of the top platform. We noticed that many parts of the temple had been vandalized and were recently restored. With the help of UNESCO it had become a listed World Heritage Site.

One day we took a becak ride in downtown Jogyakarta, southwest of Salatiga. The hard pedaling driver was a skinny, small-built man. Tom empathized with his situation and paid him more than the anticipated rate. The next time we needed a becak, we were immediately surrounded by eager drivers. We were overwhelmed by the crowd and decided to walk instead. We also visited Ubud and Denpasar in Bali. We ended our Indonesian visit at our ICA-Indonesia community in Jakarta. Tom and I learned more and more about each other as we visited this exciting variety of cultures, families, relatives, and friends. We visited Hong Kong and Tokyo before we landed in LA where Sherry Thorson, Tom's sister, warmly greeted us. We stayed with her and her family in their beautiful home in Laguna Beach. We had an American-style experience of visiting three of Tom's aunts, going to Disneyland, and sharing a spectacular BBQ at Sherry's.

The ICA-USA Summer Program, then called the ICA Global Council, was in full swing when we arrived in Chicago. It was good to see colleagues from around the world gathered to share their findings, progresses, issues, and successful ways for building a world where people could live and work together side by side. We were very pleased to learn that we were assigned to ICA-Germany and to be stationed in Frankfurt for the following two years. We spent a few days with Tom's other sister, Marilee, and her family in West Amana, Iowa, then visited with Jim, Tom's brother, in Davenport, Iowa. Our high point during that visit was a Corn Boil sponsored by the farmers of the Iowa Pork Producers Association and the Davenport Rotary Club as guests of club members, Mel and Jim Reemtsma.

The last few days were saved for Tom's parents. Our further travel took us to Detroit and Boston, where Tom had lived for two years each as staff of ICA-USA. We flew back to England and finally arrived as newlyweds in our new location in Frankfurt, Germany.

Chapter Seven

"The Power Is At the Center of the Table" is a concept of leadership that is the basis for consensus building in the ICA community reformulation work. This principle requires full participation in owning and executing a plan from each individual that makes up the group or community. The consensus building is supposed to transform the understanding of "my individual work" into a grasp of "our task." In my experience this form of transformation requires patience, courage and a continued expansion of awareness. James Hollis would call it a step into largeness. I was privileged to participate in community reformulation work at several locations across the globe including Jakarta, Amsterdam, Brussels, Frankfurt, and Toronto.

Our ICA-Frankfurt community was located on Darmstaedter Landstrasse in Frankfurt am Main, West Germany. The city of Frankfurt sits within the Main River Valley, just east of where the Main meets the Rhine.

It possesses many aspects of the old world that function as viable parts of this contemporary city. The Henninger family home, a carved red stone building built in 1898, is a well-kept historic site that our group rented from the City Hall. Near us was the Henninger Brewery that a few years ago was closed and torn down. Our neatly organized office, and enticing workshop spaces were on the first floor. One flight down was the kitchen and the cellar where vegetables, potatoes and wine were stored during the winter. The kitchen was a warm, *gemutlich* (cozy and inviting) hub that attracted everyone who wanted to hang around between meetings for a chat, cup of coffee, or glass of water. On the second and third floors were the family rooms and dorms. Tom and I occupied a room on the third floor. We could watch sunsets and the brightly lit city in the evenings from our window. In the mornings we hardly had time to watch the sunrises, since our days started at five.

One morning some of us stopped briefly in the kitchen on our way to a meeting about a healthy diet for our community. Some of us were engaged in a heated conversation about the menu of the week. Heidi, a German student in nursing and new to the community, asked, "Why can't we have more fruits and vegetables, and no white bread on our menu?" "Yes, that's the right issue. I've been asking myself that same question," said Gustav, also a German student. He continued, "What's the nutritional value of spaghetti? Why do we have to eat food that is not good for our bodies?"

We headed towards the meeting room, which was set up in a suitable and attractive fashion. Some colorful pictures of food categories were posted on one wall and healthy food charts on the other. Flyers describing balanced food combinations and total wellness were placed on the table. The ambiance was perfectly created for the topic of the meeting that day.

The leadership team, sensing dissatisfaction for some time, hoped to discuss the matter and come up with a solution. Heidi, Gustav, and David (a Canadian non-practicing-lawyer), two American women (one an ex-missionary and the other a teacher), Giselle (a German nutritionist), Ursula (a German High School senior), Mario (a young Turkish handyman) and I (an Indonesian teacher), attended the meeting. Our ages varied from 18 – 65. The meeting was held in English. Translations from English into German and vise versa were necessary for those who were struggling in either language. David our leader laid out the agenda for the meeting. To set the context, he mentioned our limited food budget, the principle of poverty, and the global aspect of our community. It was his hope to reach a consensus that included and embraced all aspects of the issue. "How can we build a healthy community by eating hamburgers, spaghetti, processed cheese, and white bread?" Gustav let out angrily. "Is this how we're supposed to demonstrate how to live as a healthy community?" Although I had come a long way in expressing my opinion, compared to previous years, listening to the blunt expressions of Gustav and others in the group made me flinch. I did not voice my opinion. I noticed Mario's sad and frightened expression. He did not say a word either. I wondered if he might be afraid that we would not have regular meals. Offended by his remark, Sarah, one of the American ladies, responded, "This is what we can afford with our current food budget. As you know, one of the principles of our community is built on living in poverty. This is one of the ways we remind ourselves that not everybody in the world has enough food to eat, let alone good food we mostly prefer." Sarah usually contributed her own funds to our community when our food budget to feed 15 people ran out. "Out of solidarity with the world we don't have to sacrifice our own health, do we?" uttered Heidi. Giselle said, "Like Americans love hamburgers, so do Germans love bratwursts; but for the sake of good health we eat less red meat, and no white bread at all." Ursula came to Sarah's rescue and explained, "We should have respect for Sarah who was willing to be in charge of the kitchen and meals with a limited budget."

David asked us to brainstorm a vision for our community. We clustered the items, named the clusters, and came up with a statement we could all accept: "Towards an Affordable, Healthy Menu for our Learning Community." Gustav who did not seem congruent with previous statements, but realizing the implications of our agreed plan said, "I am here for a limited time, only two years, to be part of this community in order to learn about the Technology of Participation (ToP) program. After that I'll join ICA-India. I certainly don't want to spend my time worrying about healthy meals although I prefer eating well." Although he was disappointed, Gustav went along.

Then David asked one of us to state our vision which led to the vision. We went through the same process: brainstorm, cluster, name, and a statement. In this case there was a conclusion: "Learning is most important to all of us." We also recommended contacting local farmers for fresh produce and bakeries for whole wheat breads. Mario, who liked to bake bread, offered to bake once a month. Gustav knew of a bakery in his hometown that could supply us with rye bread and other solid, good German breads. Sarah continued to chair the food department.

Since I traveled for my work most of the time, I did not offer any suggestions. Was this another one of my escapes? With my family's background as bakers and my experience in baking, I could have come up with some useful suggestions. Perhaps I felt disconnected from the group, or I thought my recommendations were not worth mentioning. Occasionally I still prefer to be silent. Reflecting on an event, meeting, or experience was considered an important part of our community living. It was our understanding that reflection could reveal the need for change and consider the challenges that change might bring. At the end of this meeting we participated in a reflection exercise. We asked ourselves: What happened in the meeting? How did it make us feel? What was its meaning for us? What do we need to do next? It's amazing how such a simple process of reflection enabled the healing of wounds, the affirmation of our reality, and finding ways of moving into the future!

That evening we came to the realization that although the power was at the center of the table, the individual must experience to acquire it. For me this meant daring to voice my feelings and values about the issue at hand. It took me years to dare express myself, not only in English but also in Dutch or Indonesian.

In this process of consensus building, I often experienced pressure to state a consensus before I was ready. Being brought up in a culture where obedience to leadership was of great importance I swallowed this uncomfortable reality over and over again. For years I was unable to step out of the collective mindset and remained chained by it. Gradually I came to realize that if we are unaware of this dynamic within ourselves, as leaders, we easily become dominators or oppressors within the consensus building process itself—including of ourselves.

The consensus building process became one of ICA's trademarks, a collective achievement in which we all took great pride. As part of the collective, however, the individual's creativity—for many, including mine—shriveled and did not have the chance to grow.

As for my own inner journey, I frequently found myself taking side roads and byways to procrastinate and avoided relating to myself. I loved the idea of the journey to greater awareness, but I continuously and firmly told myself that the community's task must come before anything else.

It was the end of September 1983 when we celebrated *Erntedankfest* (Harvest Festival of Thanksgiving). The Germanic Erntedankfest is primarily a rural and religious celebration and when it is held in big cities, it is part of a church service. It is unlike the big, traditional family events as in Canada and America. Our community created a North American feast with a *Gans* (the traditional goose) and a *Truthahn* (turkey) side-by-side. Gustav brought a freshly baked, two-yard long whole wheat bread loaf.

On that same day Mario taught the group how to bake Turkish rolls. Tom baked his mother's favorite recipe of caramelized ginger and orange sweet potatoes. The second floor was transformed into a festive hall with a long table in the middle. Smaller side tables were put in the corners. Colorful tablecloths from Hawaii, India, Indonesia, Japan, Taiwan, and Turkey reflected our multi-cultural community. The festivities were coordinated with taste and flair. I felt uplifted and filled with gratitude upon returning from a work trip to Vienna, Austria, where I had some reporting to do to several religious orders that supported our community reformulation projects in Africa and India.

Regularly I wrote to Aunt Ellie describing what I did, and had seen of the different countries and cultures. She responded by telling me how much Mother would have appreciated my work, and how proud she was of me. Aunt Ellie could hardly believe that I did exactly what Mother had wished to do herself. It reminded me of what Irene Claremont de Castillejo, author and Jungian psychotherapist, said in Knowing Woman, that a mother lived again in the daughter and the little girl lived mother's life and shared her activities from the moment she could act at all.

The ICA community designed a good decision-making

process, but the individual had to make it one's own if it were to be meaningful. I was not used to letting contrary ideas exist side-by-side. When I disagreed with someone else's idea, I tended to fight the other's idea. In my limited way of expression, both linguistically as well as psychologically, I found it easier to walk away from reality. I was not up for the battle. It took me awhile to learn to live in close proximity with another who did not share my ideas. We were an inclusive community of individuals who respected and allowed each other to participate in making decisions that concerned the whole. This was the community that Joe Mathews had envisioned.

Gradually Tom and I began to realize that we had developed a unique bond. Living as a couple was a new experience. We were two individuals from different cultural and personal backgrounds. We had to learn to know and to love each other and ourselves. This was not an easy task. As newly-weds, living in a community, and immersed in concentrated teamwork, we had little time with, or for, each other except on what we called family night, a six-hour block of time on Thursdays. We adapted to our community rule: to put our mission first, beyond our personal needs. Only gradually did we learn to relate to each other as spouses. Others supported our adjustment to our relationship, for which we continue to be grateful.

Yet my individual journey was a solo project as was Tom's. Having people around diverted our full attention to each other in a positive way as their presence made the adjustment to each other more gradual. During our first years of marriage, we tried hard to contain explosive emotions but eruptions happened anyway. I was easily irritated when I perceived that Tom was uncommitted to our union. I assumed jealous attitudes towards other women who snagged Tom's attention. Sometimes I was just mad at life.

One Saturday afternoon I was assigned to our children's program. Meanwhile I had planned to pick up my glasses at the optician's. Since an assigned task had priority over personal plans and needs, another ICA staff was assigned to pick them up, but arrived later empty handed. I was furious! As a result I threw a flowerpot from one end of the office to the other. An uncontrollable anger overcame me. No one was hurt except for the African violets. I felt badly about the flowers, but also felt a deliberate lack of respect of the other by not getting the glasses when I expected them. No one seemed to be bothered by not keeping promises they made. I had to learn to sacrifice personal needs for the sake of fulfilling a larger mission. Tom picked them up the following Monday.

The following pantoum describes Tom's and my relationship to each other at that time. A pantoum is one of the old, traditional forms of poetry that has its root in Chinese and Persian literature. It is also a Malayan form of poetry from the fifteenth century. In Indonesia this form is still widely used. Unique to the form is the repeats of the second and fourth lines of each stanza in the following stanza. Repeating those lines gives an effect of weaving similar ideas into and through the whole poem. Kim Addonizio and Dorianne Laux described this form in *The Poet's Companion.*

In Poperinge, Belgium, we meet
as strangers to each other and ourselves.
On this journey of great discovery
within ourselves and outer world.

A stranger to myself, I understand
of being lost, circling the same track over and over.
He, in Luxembourg, misses the train.
I, in Sydney, scared, lose my way home.

Over and over again the same trail.
I stop and reflect along the waters.
Scared, lost, we long for the familiar.
We must find the way home ourselves.

Along the river Rhine we reflect, celebrate
our first anniversary of marriage.
He, I, each must find the way back home
after having been lost so many times.

Our anniversary in a motorboat.
almost sunk near Koln,
Lost so many times, we keep up the struggle
to find the path to the Self; his core, my core.

We are saved and freed by acceptance
on the journey of great discovery.
Recognize who we are: opposites.
In Poperinge, Belgium, we meet.

In the midst of consolidating the concensus building process our bond developed. The relationship between the two of us changed as we individually learned to accept ourselves. After having been in Europe for eight years it was about time to take up another assignment. North America was our next possibility of destiny.

Chapter Eight

To leave Europe meant parting with a culture I was familiar with since childhood. North America was not completely foreign to me, but it was a culture I did not know well. There was that eagerness to discover that 'otherness' that attracts and at the same time the frightening question: "What is in store for me there?" After a week in Toronto, I returned to Frankfurt for three weeks to pack up and really say goodbye to the environment I loved. I felt sadness and grief, combined with a pull to the future.

In Toronto we lived in a three-story building with nine family units in an area called, The Beaches. I liked the area for its history, the mix of artists, students, and people of all ages who fill the streets. Our building is just a few minutes walk north from Lake Ontario. Concerts, jazz festivals, art & craft shows were annually held at a nearby park, called Kew Gardens. Streetcars ran from five in the morning till midnight from The Beaches all the way through downtown and on west to High Park. On Saturdays Tom and I would walk to our favorite gourmet coffee shop for breakfast or brunch. The winters were very cold, long, and unbearable at times.

Nov. 7, 1984, just a month after I came back from Frankfurt, my sister Maud passed away at 50 after a long, ugly battle with ovarian cancer. I thought of her quite often and regretted we were miles apart, not only physically, but also in our thinking. I had just begun to discover who I really was and to search for the other in myself. Terrified by the tyranny that ignorance and superstition left us with I was totally helpless. Soon followed more sad news: Valerie died on May 20, 1985 at the age of 55 also from an undetected ovarian cancer. I was completely devastated—numb. Not a single tear could I squeeze from my eyes. I'd lost the capacity to grieve. Recently I read Dara Marks' *Inside Story*. How delighted I was with her statement, that a death experience is extremely important in an effort of undoing old value systems. Indeed that experience challenged me to let go of what was obsolete and surrender to that part that was struggling to be born. However, the experience of being left alone was miserable. We had a long winter that year. It snowed right to early May. Grieving over my sisters' deaths during those long winter months stimulated a deep longing for the warmth of spring and new life. Tom was gracious, gentle, and understanding in those dark and difficult days. We decided to visit the families of Maud and Valerie the following year.

The deaths of my two sisters in such a short time span was

a wake-up call for me to pay serious attention to my own health. Tom and I committed ourselves to regular exercise and eating well. For a while we were strict vegetarians. No red meat appeared on our daily menu until we visited and stayed with Tom's parents one summer where we had meat almost every day. When we returned home we allowed red meat back for just one time a week. We then fanatically followed the "Fit for Life" diet, which taught us among others about food combinations.

Each one of us built a personal regimen that worked best for us. My morning jogs were also a way to get acquainted with the neighborhood. I enjoyed noticing the neat little gardens with tulips of many colors along the way to the lake. We took dance and yoga classes for many years. Spiritual, psychological, physical well-being was important to us, and still is.

June 1986. On our way to Indonesia, Tom and I stopped in Hawaii for two days. After the cold, winter months of Toronto, the spring weather of Honolulu was refreshing and inviting for a stroll on the beach.

So much had changed since 1982, Tom's first visit to my family. In Jakarta we paid a visit to Cilincing, Java Sea where Maud's ashes were scattered and had a picnic lunch at the white sand beach. We paid tribute to Valerie's grave in Salatiga. How grateful I was to see new life being carried by Valerie's oldest daughter. A new generation was in sight. They named him Adhi Utomo. Now a graphic designer, he edited the pictures printed in this book.

Five years later in Toronto I was overjoyed to see my nephew Hauw, who is also called Budhianto--Valerie's son--who arrived on a business trip from Indonesia en route to Europe in the spring of 1991. I have relatives after all! He stayed with us for a week. We took him to the Canadian side of the Niagara Falls, and to see the McMichael Canadian Art Gallery in Kleinberg, Ontario, which featured a collection of paintings of the Group of Seven that is most famous for its Canadian landscapes. The gallery also displays Emily Carr's painting. Although closely associated with the Group of Seven, she was never an official member. I was pleased Hauw appreciated Emily Carr's paintings too. Most of all I treasured just being with him. Hauw has now taught English as a second language in Indonesia for over 25 years. These days he teaches ESL teachers. Together with his three sisters they provided medical care and social security for their aging father who died in 2011. Hauw is a living example of a son who is his parents' pride. He reminded me of my mother's greatest fear for not having a son who could care for her in old age. As I am writing this memoir I am so grateful for his efforts in recovering special family data and photographs.

I traveled quite regularly for ICA-Canada as I had during my European assignments. There were religious orders in Vancouver, Winnipeg, Edmonton, Montreal, Quebec City and Toronto who supported our community reformulation projects in India and Africa. My business meetings with the Provincial Superiors were usually short and I was very pleased to visit with the retired nuns and priests who had worked in Indonesia and elsewhere in the world as missionaries. They had so much to tell about those countries, the people, and their work. Not only did we reminisce about the good old times, but we shared experiences of our inner journeys as well. When we visited Montreal, Tom and I stayed with Father Jansen who entertained us with his life stories. He told us how he learned from his mother to cook oatmeal porridge the right way. In his younger years as a priest he taught school and did not have the chance to work in the kitchen. Then in his eighties, and as his community became smaller, he had cooked regularly for five retired priests. He loved to travel by the underground trains and he showed us around Old Montreal where artists had their exhibits. He shared many of his personal stories of adjustments made in his life. For instance, how authoritarian he was as a young priest in Indonesia: always the leader who knew what was best in every situation of life on earth and beyond. He regretted how limiting he had been by not allowing discussion with others who were related to many of his projects.

The 1984 ICA International Summer Program, held in Chicago, opened with a spiritual journey exercise based on the story of the Wizard of Oz facilitated by Jean Houston. It was an exercise designed for individuals as part of a group. The challenge for all of us was how to take up our own journey towards full consciousness individually. Like the rest, so must I find the shoes that fit my feet. As the individuals' awareness expands, a growing need for reconstructing emerged. ICA-International including ICA-Canada, decided that it was time to reconstruct itself. Each one of us was offered the opportunity to redefine our relationship to ICA and its mission. Across the globe people felt the necessity to stand on their own feet as local ICAs or individuals. Tom and I decided to step out of the community and continue to live in Toronto. Although we are dispersed over the globe, our bond between individuals remains in tact. Jim Wiegel--team member of the global community reformulation projects—lives with his wife, Judith, in Tolleson. I deeply appreciated his wise counsel as I wrote about my experiences with ICA-International. I am also grateful to Yvonne Ford in Germany who e-mailed me her view on my German experience.

Three major changes lay ahead of me: to take up a

new job at the age of sixty, to consolidate a family, and to discover the self I was meant to be.

I got certified in Wellness and Lifestyle Management from Centennial College and took up a job as Senior Services Director at a community center in Scarborough. Tom took several courses in gerontology at the Centennial College, and found a part-time job at a senior center that provided personal care to male seniors living in their own homes. It was at the Seniors' Centre where I discovered the need for a life review for older adults. I designed a six-session Life Review workshop. The intent of the workshop was to review one's life by recalling the past, stating the present and discerning glimpses of the future. This was done through writing and telling our life stories, painting, and Buddhist meditation.

A ritual for crossing a threshold from one to another phase of our life seemed to be appropriate and appreciated. I did mine for my 60th birthday.

I invited my Jungian analyst friend from Boston to facilitate this ritual. She helped me re-experience my birth as a female baby who was warmly welcomed by her women friends. The re-entry ritualized a shift from a rejected platform to an accepted stage. Did the absence of my mother, pressure me to mother myself, to give birth to spirit as she give birth to my body? After the ritual we walked through the park to a recreation center where we joined our spouses and celebrated my birthday with champagne, an Indonesian dinner, and a delicious three-layered cake. To toast our vibrant lives all participants were invited to light a candle in honor of their own individual lives and communities. We continued the evening with dancing and conversations. We had a great time.

Tom and I were not quite used to each other yet, and were still learning to be a couple. Not only were we strangers to one another, but most of all we were strangers to ourselves. That made getting to know each other more urgent, interesting and difficult.

One evening I had steamed tofu, baked wild rice pilaf and walnuts. I planned to steam some green beans a few minutes before Tom was expected home. Fifteen, thirty, sixty minutes passed. There was no Tom, nor was there a phone call letting me know where he was. My anxiety, disappointment, and anger grew wilder by the minute. I had a lecture ready for him: "A good husband ought to be home by dinner time. If you will be late, you should call me, and tell me exactly when you will be home." He finally arrived home—to my great surprise—with a big, beautiful, black dog that seemed to be lost and needed a place to stay. Tom easily felt sympathy for all lost, poor, and destitute beings. Overwhelmed by the dog's feeling of being lost, he was in a quandary, and finally decided to bring him home. I was flabbergasted and said furiously: "You ought to be committed to me first and not to a dog!" Generalizations, slogans, conventional ideas and Mother's opinion about good husbands suddenly flashed through my mind. Both of us were shocked, hurt, and felt misunderstood. Such an outburst just happened. It felt as if I was at the mercy of an uncontrollable energy. We let the beautiful dog stay for the night. The next morning Tom took her to the closest animal care center.

The first ten years of our marriage were very uncomfortable years. At times I did not know what to do to make our relationship less stressful. My urge for control grew with each new challenge in our relationship. Living together daily as a couple left us with the otherness of the other. We were like strangers to ourselves and to each other. I had been pretending all my life to be someone else in order to be accepted by others—first by my mother, by other relatives, and society at large. I had denied my own womanhood and imperfect hand. I was unhappy with myself and our relationship.

Tom could occasionally be moody, depressed, and indecisive. He is at heart an eternal youth and is used to hiding in his fantasy world where he felt safe, secure, and protected from the real world of sometimes very cruel demands and commitments. He too was not happy with our bond and with himself.

Lawrence Staples, a Jungian analyst and author of *The Creative Soul* wrote about the need for mirroring as a yearning for the self. I was attracted to and repelled from Tom at the same time. Staples reminded me that in Tom I saw my own deep longing for that which I had pushed away all my life. It was in my relationship to Tom that I would find my true self, the one that I was meant to be.

We were planning to go to the library one day. He was moody and rather depressive that morning and completely forgot our appointment. How could he forget! I was disappointed and furious! Tom, too, was at the end of his rope. He grabbed a flowerpot of cyclamen in full bloom and smashed it on the floor. He felt guilty and left our apartment. Alone I screamed and cried. I was in a quandary: single life was unbearable and so was married life. Finally, at my wit's end, I dropped down on my knees and surrendered to the unknown—a force that was greater than myself.

Later that day Tom came home and we discussed our situation and decided to seek help. The following week, we each went into individual Jungian analysis. I had reconnected with the work of Carl Gustav Jung, whom I first came across during my undergraduate studies in pedagogy in Jakarta in 1958. Jung, a depth psychologist, was concerned with the psychic and spiritual worlds that were hidden from us, buried in the darkness of the unknown—the unconscious. In addition Tom took classes at George Brown College in Working with Adult Children of Alcoholics & Co-dependents.

We both began to realize that each one of us should continue to work on ourselves if we treasured our bond. Within our relationship of two opposites I must find my true self, the one that I was meant to be. Only after learning to accept and respect our unique selves, was living our life together possible. The journey, however, had to be taken individually. We saw this as our lifelong task.

Another thing I learned was that anything that negatively or positively stirs me deeply must be taken seriously. I had the following dream, which I took into an analysis session:

> I find my hibiscus plant in a pot at the center of my house. It has grown out of the pot and become a tree. The branches grow up to the ceiling. The irregular sized, red hibiscus flowers bloom. The roots spread and crack the pot into pieces. Some of the roots are badly damaged.

I woke up sad and bewildered. Surely the plant needed more space for its full growth to take place. It seemed to me that the dream was my soul's reminder of the situation I was in which required my full attention.

I recalled the first hibiscus plant in our married life. Tom and I received a beautiful deep-red hibiscus plant as a gift on our wedding day in Brussels. We took it with us when we moved to Frankfurt, Germany, but we had to leave that beautiful plant behind when we moved to Toronto. We bought a new one. Exploring the process of repotting my new hibiscus plant into a larger container, I purchased a bigger clay pot and a bag of fertilized soil. I gave my full attention to the hibiscus plant for several days. First, I poured fresh water into the soil and let it soak. Then carefully I loosened up the soil to free the roots and discover new ones. While taking the plant out of the old pot and shaking the dirt off the roots, I discovered a few damaged ones. Replanting the hibiscus in a new pot was an unusually painful experience resulting in an expansive and insecure feeling. The hibiscus tree grows well in Indonesia. It likes full sunlight and heat. In Europe, my experience with a hibiscus plant was that it needed the sunniest and warmest spot in the room. My experience with the hibiscus plant was a metaphor for my inner growth. I learned that the soul couldn't be confined by rules and dogmas, but needs to freely grow into continuously expanding environments.

As I gained more confidence on the path of greater consciousness I had another dream:

> I sit, reading a book on the sofa in our living room. Suddenly three kittens are placed on my lap. They are jumping and dancing around and coming at me.

I woke up, overwhelmed, frightened at first. What was I supposed to do with those kittens? I was just beginning to learn about my feminine energy—the kittens. They wanted to get to know me as much as I wanted to get to know them. But their playfulness frightened me. Tom said, after listening to my dream: "Kittens do you no harm. They just want you to dance, have fun, and be playful. There is no dogma or rules for loosening up."

I also have learned that these images are sacred. When in analysis I was dealing with the boxed-in tree in the apartment of my dream mentioned earlier, I felt a deep recognition of something personal and intimate that was not fully explainable. The encounter left me with a feeling of awe. I had much to learn from this point of view, and so did Tom.

Looking at my dream of the dancing kittens, he immediately pointed to the sharp claws they might have. How painful that could be when used to attack someone. Another facet he saw was that the dream portrayed kittens, instead of cats. The jumping and rolling of the kittens called for playful participation. Tom's imagery is colorful, expansive, and delightful and helps me imagine complex psychological realities. What I still needed to understand was the number three in this dream. It seemed that it reminded me of a third reality that had been created between two opposites, the masculine and the feminine within me, and between Tom and I.

Tom had not taken the time to develop the beautiful gift of imagery then. Now he cherishes the new energies, ideas, and images and brings them to visual life. Tom loves to cook. He likes the feel of soft fabric, the smell of exotic fragrances. He adores the shapes, colors, and fragrances of flowers. The animal world fascinates him. Unfortunately, he could not pursue these interests while growing up as they were not the generally approved masculine traits required for development into manhood. Instead he buried them in his unconscious and this became his personal shadow. By calling up these hidden traits to his attention, he took an important step toward becoming whole.

Slowly, Tom and I came to understand that in order for us to be in a relationship as equals, we had to be individually mature to accept and love ourselves as we are, and let the opposites within ourselves dance.

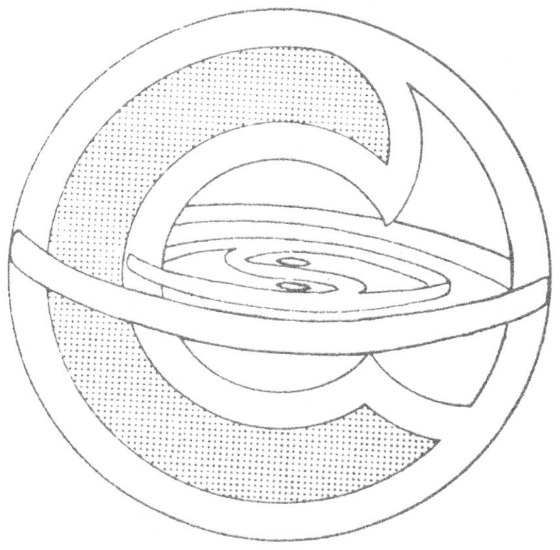

The inner circle illustrates the yin-yang in ourselves,
the horizontal eclipse points to the yin-yang of our
relationship to one another. The whole ball refers to the
yin-yang of our relationship to all there is.

We conceptualized and described in our marriage document that first, individually, then as a couple, and lastly in our relationship to all there is, we are a totality of Yin-Yang. The Yin-Yang or feminine/masculine opposites do not only apply in ourselves, but also in our marriage and our community. As time passed we learned that consensus building also requires mature individuals to at least prevent one having control over the other.

Becoming aware of and understanding what the unconscious tried to tell me was one thing; integrating these newly gained insights into my life was another. Accepting myself as a woman with a crippled hand was key to accepting Tom just as he was.

Setbacks on the journey were also part of my experience. One setback was when I had to leave the senior services of the Community Centre where I worked, because of my inability to harness my drive to impose new attitudes on the staff before they were ready to accept and implement them. I recognized that I still had not honed the ability to receive, consider others' contributions, and input of potential ideas. I am sure there always will be setbacks in the future.

In the midst of resistance to my new ideas, I recognized ongoing support from a few colleagues who believed in me and in the new ideas I introduced to the center. I facilitated the celebration of a 90-year-old lady, Mrs. Stein, who claimed her beautiful life of service as a nurse. There were rumors from people around her who raised questions such as, "How could you initiate and invite others to your own birthday party? Is that not a self-serving and sinful gesture?" Mrs. Stein was of the opinion that claiming one's life—which that event was—meant taking responsibility for it. She did not see anything sinful in her initiative.

Instead the celebration of her life was an opportunity to express gratitude for her life of service to others. As for me, I felt that by supporting Mrs. Stein to claim her life of service, I had offered her and others the opportunity to seize a new possibility to live life to the fullest. I was filled with gratitude to continue what I had started. A good crowd of people came to the celebration. We sat in a circle. When the time came for her to read her life story, she stood up, confident and strong. She then was asked to go through a self-made gate she helped to decorate. Mrs. Stein stepped elegantly over the threshold, and then appeared startled! On the other side of the gate, some friends welcomed her including the doubters. Symbolically she had entered a new phase in her life. It was an awesome moment. I admired her courage to go through the ritual despite those who discounted her motivation.

To take up a new job at sixty was not as challenging as to make a shift from a control freak to one who was loyal to herself and at the same time loyal to the other.

Tom and I bought our first home, a condominium, in Scarborough, a suburb of Toronto. As time passed, Tom's parents, brother, and two sisters came and stayed with us at different times. We enjoyed them so much. Over the years, our German, Dutch and Australian friends have come to visit and stay with us. But after living through sixteen long, cold winters, we yearned for the warmth of the sun. Tom, who had to shovel many feet of snow every winter, wanted to return to Arizona. Before he went to Europe he had lived in Phoenix, and since 1983 we visited his parents in Sun City West, Arizona for Christmas every other year. The warmth of Arizona appealed to us. We enjoyed helping his father set up the luminarias which are little candles put in brown paper bags filled with some scoops of sand and were put a yard apart from each other along the street in front of their house and driveway. On Christmas Eve just before dark, we lit them. It was such a delightful scene. The whole community participated in letting their little lights shine. It was indeed a wonderful example of a community effort.

The weather and the alluring environment of the desert drew me. For three years we lived in Sun City, Arizona, for half the year and the other half in Toronto. It was only in 2000 that we headed to the desert to find a permanent home where we continue to learn to hold the tension between opposites within ourselves, between each other, and between the outer world and ourselves.

Chapter Nine

Something about the desert compels me to explore. As a young girl I was fascinated by the 40 years of wandering in the desert of the Israelites. During those years the Israelites experienced disappointments as well as fulfillments and blessings. Jesus and other spiritual leaders like Buddha and Mahatma Gandhi regularly sought the desert for inner dialogue and restoration. What is it about the desert that attracts yet frightens me, I often ask.

Since we moved to the desert 15 years ago almost every morning I walk the streets in my neighborhood just to get a feel for its energy. It invites me to observe, to ponder not only my outer reality, but my inner life as well. It is the stillness through which I learn to hear the long sought voice of soul.

I've become acqainted with a variety of cacti. They are so different in sort and size. The most well known in our area are the saguaro, cholla, and ocotillo. We have a prickly pear cactus in our front yard where rabbits find their shelter and homes. The golden yellow flowers that grow at the top have a diameter of two inches. They come out in the spring and, when open, the blooms look like a tiny green toad cupped in a child's hand.

One day I watched a woodpecker carving a nest in a tall, strong saguaro, a scene you would not see in a busy cosmopolitan city like Toronto. The bird was just happy that I gave him attention. A white-winged dove who reminded me of Dara—Grandma's dove—visited daily. She sat right in front of my window. Every morning, when I opened the window blinds and turned on my computer, I'd find her perched on the windowsill to wish me good luck with my writing. She encouraged me to get at it even when occasionally it could get very tough. I missed her when she did not come anymore because the summer became too hot for her.

The male Costa's humming birds that usually visit us in the spring have a purple iridescence on their throats and crowns. They love blooming honeysuckle. Another common bird in our area is the chihuahuan raven, often featured in Native American myths. It has black, shiny feathers, with a wedge shaped tail. One day I watched one sharing an orange with a rabbit in our back yard.

Rabbits search for sprouting plants before the day gets too hot. Proud quails with their young enjoy their morning walks just like me. Once a lizard surprised me on my path. A rattlesnake gliding smoothly through the stem of bushes and trees can be a scary experience and gives me goose bumps even now as I write.

Sometimes a sudden sand storm swirls right in front of me, blinding my eyes. Occasionally, a sharp, heated beam of sunlight slices through the air. In these situations all we can do is just wait, and let the storm run its course. This is the desert wisdom that Dennis Slattery writes about, that in the desert every plant, animal, insect seems to know what is needed to adapt, to adjust, to conserve, to move with a slow, graceful pace or a quick jerky one. It's like recovering from a bad fall at the age of 75, when I just could not hurry the healing process of my bruised muscles. In the midst of waiting for the injury to heal that took more than six months, I did yoga.

I have read about the wildness of the desert, but never observed it so closely. Here I learned to be grateful for the smallest and simplest joys, such as watching roadrunners that prefer to strut or run across the street with a lizard or a little snake in their beaks, rather than fly. Every time I see one crossing the road I stop and let her stride with pride before I continue my walk. It is a delightful experience to watch her. Living in the desert helped me listen to the voice that wanted to be heard.

Myths that people live by fascinated me. I felt a growing need to get certified in mythic memoir writing. I applied—I was seventy then—and in 2001, I was interviewed and accepted for a Ph.D program in Mythological Studies at Pacifica Institute for Graduate Studies. I was euphoric! On my flight home from Santa Barbara while mulling over the possibility of taking up that program, a European fairy tale called Vrouw or Frau Holle came to mind. Frau Holle used to sit at her well. One day a girl, who had skipped school, walked by the well. She stopped, looked into the well, and somehow dropped her ring in it. She jumped into the well to find her precious ring. When she stood up from the fall she found herself in a garden full of fruit trees and flowers of various kinds. She walked through the garden, looked around, and was delighted and pleased with what she found. In the deeps of the well she found unlimited possibilities of nourishment and beauty.

Like the girl in that story I pursued a wish that led me to a completely different experience. I wanted to participate in the Pacifica Institute's Mythological Studies very much, but realized the looming financial obligation was unjustifiable. I let go of the Pacifica dream and continued leading workshops from home, reading and writing, attending workshops of interest, and finding my own community. No matter how much I wanted to get a Ph.D, the universe apparently didn't agree with me, and it was pinching me through finances to keep me on another path. That seemed so unfair—it hurt. But it was necessary for me to skip study, drop my precious ring, and jump into the well so I could fall down a mythic well where Frau Holle herself could find and mentor me. I interpret that Frau Holle embodies the wise woman who is the keeper of the well, and the wisdom of the depths. Elf owls that nest in a saguaro in the backyard of our friends in Tucson represent that subtle wisdom, humility, and graciousness. I found my own community and was guided by the wise feminine herself. I began to search for the new and unexplored in my life and see reality with new eyes.

Gradually I discovered other possibilities of learning. I wrote poetry for six years with several women between the ages of 70 and 80. Our poetry circle met twice a month and we had so much fun writing and reading our work. We submitted our work to poetry magazines. Some of them were published which made us proud and encouraged us to continue writing. We did presentations on poetry writing at two local churches in Sun City. We also wrote stories about our pasts, reflected on our experiences, and tried to understand the purposes of our individual and collective lives. We came to the United States from different parts of the world and cultural backgrounds. Some of us arrived in this country when we were young and others came as adults. Heartbreaking stories were shared. Ann Helen, a charming Polish lady, recalled how she had to change her Polish name in order to get a job as a teacher in Massachusetts. Her story reminded a Russian born Canadian friend, Kira Kremer, and me about our similar experiences. In the late 60s as I sat for my master's degree exam in Amsterdam, I had to change my Chinese name, Tan Kwie Hwa into Deborah Connie Widyatma, as suggested by a friend. Twelve years later, I got married and became Deborah Connie Reemtsma.

Others in the group, who grew up during the Great Depression, remembered their childhood memories about money difficulties. The melodies of Christian hymns and other comforting songs softened the suffering like a cozy favorite blanket. Wanda remembered Love's Old Sweet Song (Molloy, J.L.1837-1909) that she and her mother used to sing: "Tho' the heart be weary, sad the day and long/Still to us at twilight comes Love's old song, Love's old sweet song."

Memories of my own childhood and dealing with the effects of polio awakened in me a realization of how blessed I was. Through my deformity I have learned to interact with my body. My body's knowing has guided me throughout the years.

Marilyn, a performing artist, is a woman whom I admire for her courage. At the age of 80, while reflecting on her life, she realized that she was taught that her beauty and attractiveness were dangerous assets and was encouraged to suppress them. As she matured she courageously claimed her gifts and learned to take full responsibility for them.

These women, now in their late 80's, wealthy and healthy, expressed their gratitude for life. It seemed that the importance of telling, writing, and sharing our stories was to recognize the transformation that had taken place within each of us. Enormous rewards of deep satisfaction resulted from the risks Tom and I took to uncover deeper truths about ourselves in relationship. When I used to pretend that I was emotionally strong and yet was not, all my energy was utilized to defend myself and to rationalize my actions. It felt as if I did not have time for anything else but worrying about all things. By gradually accepting who I really am, my energy is now available for creative activities, such as initiating a memoir-writing circle or ritualizing significant events. It gave me deep satisfaction. That was the inner marriage that Woodman was talking about. It was by holding the tension of opposites that a third, new reality came into being.

In our poetry circle I wrote this poem:

The Beauty of Autumn

before the leaves are swept away
into winter
autumn displays one last brilliant flair
of outrageous colors

as I feel forewarnings of old age
I usher in
my own autumn of brilliance
as I gather and enjoy the fruits of my reflective life

Tom continues to develop his personal trainer skills for the older adult while keeping an eye on the path of becoming and accepting the reality of who he is. Gradually through accepting myself, I have stopped insisting who he needs to be or how he should act, as I had in the past. My longing for the other, the inner marriage, and the pleasure I found in writing has made me less critical of myself as well as of Tom.

The desert also inspires me to sing again. I have been singing in the choir of the Unitarian Universalist Church of Surprise, Arizona led by Dr. James Flom who passed away in June 2010. Nancy Bechtolt, her late husband, Richard Bechtolt, and a few other church members started this choir a few years ago. As any other choir director, Jim expected each of us to sight-read music. The reality is that not all of us were music literates. Fortunately he accepted us as we were, and possessed an extraordinary capacity to take us to higher levels of singing.

At rehearsals he would say, "Here is a very tempting spot for screeching. That is where you don't want to go. So watch out." Or, "let's not breathe after love and power since we tend to linger on those whole notes anyway."

He had a good ear for pronunciation, which added to the excellent production of a sound. He was always looking for pure sound. Pure sound reminds me of finding an authentic, unique, personal voice in life or when singing words, voice and feeling are blended together. "Keep the rhythm, rather than prolonging a note unnecessarily," he often reminded us. Jim had an ability to keep each one of us on our toes. "A quarter note still needs to be sung, not swallowed."

In the spring of 2010 we had our first instrumental and vocal concert. Jim put together works of Bach, Bolling, Faure, Kander, Webber, and Wilson. The piano and vocal duets, and solos were delightful. The choral music covered works of Mary Lynn Lightfoot, Rollo Dilworth, Ken Medema, and Jay Althouse. I learned anew how to monitor my own singing and detect errors, correcting them as I went along. It is good to be an independent chorister, but equally important for the good of the group as a whole, is to listen to other singers and match my voice to that of the group. Jim paid close attention to important details. Somehow I experience singing as an opportunity to explore the invisible, to step on the line between the familiar and untouched areas. When our voices came together, even for just a fleeting moment, it felt as if I had arrived at the threshold where mind and soul meet. At that moment a flow of vitality swept through me and I was feeling and communicating beauty. Often I long for those dear and precious moments. The experience of singing has always held a deep and long lasting satisfaction for me. We performed, and we did it superbly. I was deeply grateful to Jim that in the short time he was conductor of our choir, he was able to take us to that level of expression. In singing I learn anew to fulfill the call of beauty. I love singing in the choir again, after having been quiet for over thirty years.

I have loved singing since my primary school days. During the war we did not sing much at Grandma's house. After the war I started music classes at the Teacher's College. I regretted there was not more time for music, which was considered a luxury in those years. I felt I had to rush to catch up with the basics and to graduate. The years after WWII were consumed with getting a diploma and finding a job. Years later I bought a mini Steinway, and play when people were not around to watch me. I took private classes in vocalization from Catherine Leimena, an Italian trained Indonesian opera singer and music teacher in Jakarta. I sang in the choruses as a mezzo soprano.

I became a member of an American Indonesian Choir Group in Jakarta. The choir conductor was Dr. Richard Haskin, an American theologian and music teacher. He was a professor at a Theological Seminary in Jakarta and lived with his family in Indonesia for over twenty years. There were about 80 international singers from several parts of the world sharing the same passion for vocal music. We performed Mozart's Requiem, Messiah, Amahl and the Night Visitors, Il Trovatore, and Carmina Burana among others; two productions a year—for Easter and Christmas. We had so much fun rehearsing and performing, while creating global friendships.

About mid-course of rehearsing Il Trovatore, we spent some time discussing costumes, make up, and performing itself. A professional stage manager was brought in to help us with our performing style. He was pleased with the gypsy and tavern scenes, and then focused on a scene in which we were performing as nuns. I could tell from his facial expression he was not too impressed with what he saw. To get a deeper sense of a nun's life-style, and to improve our performance for that particular scene, he recommended that we visit a convent before our next rehearsal. There we encountered a natural expression of awe, of being captured by something of great value. The great success of our public performance reflected our new and improved expression of an unfamiliar lifestyle. A long-standing ovation after that particular scene was a token of appreciation from the audience. It was a fulfilling experience.

I loved discovering and developing my singing voice. Unfortunately it did not last long. When I became a member of the ICA, I stopped singing the classical, conventional way. As a revolutionary—create and adopt a new style—community we did away with reading music and instead we listened to a tune, then created our own verse to that tune. We composed and sang our own inspirational songs using familiar melodies. It took a while to get used to it, but gradually I came to enjoy our ICA community singing. One of the songs that I cherish is the following:

At the Center

(Tune: Try to Remember)
When you encounter the joy at the center,
your tingling deeps in animation,
When you're possessed by the joy at the center,

all things received by affirmation,
When you are speechless in joy at the center,
and each moment brimming with wild vibration,
Then at the center, in wonder-filled rapture, you be it.

(from: ICA Community Songbook)

I am finding back my singing self that connects me with the Self.

The longing for the other was intensified and found its expression in the stillness of the desert. I recalled what John O'Donohue, author of *Beauty: The Invisible Embrace* wrote about the inner voice of the soul. He said that our task is to learn to hear the voice of our own soul. The more we learn to listen deeply, the greater the surprises and discoveries will unfold. He stated that music and silence are like lovers who gaze at each other and long for each other. Vocal music is a homecoming for me. This happens when I dare to travel to a level where the deep silence of my soul resides.

The same thing happens when in writing I express my own inner voice. It is there that I am home. Inspired by a weekend workshop on "The Art of Writing" led by Dr. Dennis Slattery at Pacifica Institute for Graduate Studies in 2007, I took an online writing memoir class offered by Deb Everson-Borofka. Her presentation of the muses was inspiring and inviting, and her writing style was warm. One of the muses to whom I related best was Urania. I have learned that Urania is the muse who inspires new discoveries, insights, inventions, Aha moments, and motivates us to pursue what beckons. I thought of Saraswati, a Hindu goddess, who, in Indonesia, is regarded as the goddess of Art, Science, and Culture. She is imagined like a river, as the flowing one, and is one of the most celebrated goddesses from the Vedic period through current times. She is portrayed having four arms; and the most common items held in her hands are a book, a lute, a rosary, and a water pot. Surely Everson-Borofka got me writing.

The following year I felt I needed a mentor. I was introduced to Dr. Jacqueline Feather, through the Institute for Cultural Change. Jacqui patiently walked me through exercises to meet, recognize, and appreciate the archetypes that had left unique patterns in my soul. I was awe struck. This journey concluded with a weekend memoir-writing workshop skillfully crafted and presented by Christine Downing, Maureen Murdock, and Jacqueline herself. It was a fabulous and inspiring weekend.

Memoir writing is an act of memory directed to the future, teaches Dennis Slattery. I collected all I had written throughout the years, more than ten years of writing. Through writing my story, I recalled not only the past, but also discovered among others the neglected parts of myself—the positive and the negative—that demanded full attention. It had taken me years to transform that orphaned girl with a defected left hand into a confident woman memoirist.

It would have been appropriate, I thought, to have the completion of the memoir ritualized around my 80th birthday. It did not happen. I grieved. A year later I discovered something else wanted to be included. At about the same time phone calls and emails came from relatives and friends in Indonesia, the Netherlands, Germany, and Australia inquiring when my memoir finally will be available.

May 29, 2012, our 30th wedding anniversary. Tom and I thought to celebrate it by inviting Ginette Paris to speak about her newest book *Heartbreak: New Approaches to Healing*. I presented this idea to several friends who were interested in Jungian thought and we had her here in Sun City on April 12, 2012. One of the supporters was the late Marlene Hall. A year ago she indicated interest in my Jungian study group. In the fall of 2011 she attended the group that studied James Hollis' *What Matters Most* that I led. On March 27, it was her turn to lead the session on "That we accept at last that Our Home is our Journey, and our Journey is our Home." She was deeply grateful to reconnect with her soul through our study together. Marlene resigned from many activities she had been involved in for many years and used that freed up time for deep listening. That's what mattered most to her. To care for Bob, her ailing husband, became the focus of her involvement. Although she sensed the topic 'Heartbreak' was not of any use to her, she wanted to participate in hosting Ginette Paris. Before she left for the summer to Afton, Oklahoma, she thanked me again for the opportunity to discern what matters most to her. Her sudden death on June 9, 2012 came as a shock. Another heartbreak.

On April 17, 2012 I found out that Rens v. Netten, maid of honor at our wedding, discovered she had ovarian cancer. She passed away in the Netherlands on May 15, 2012 at 85. I was heartbroken. In the last five years Rens and I shared our experiences of how we were victims of a wrong way of living for a long, long time. A theologian and psychologist all her adult life, she had kept herself hostage until five years ago, when she discovered in analysis what she had done to herself. She regretted that the therapy had ended and wished to have it prolonged. I regret she could not claim victor over her own imprisonment, but I deeply appreciate and salute her efforts to refuse to die a victim in her late years. Did not Jung say, "it's not to achieve the goal, but the opus that mattered?"

Ginette Paris' address at James Hillman's memorial was about 'The Art of Dying,' a topic Hillman had written about. She mentioned that rising and falling is a rhythm of life. How one falls or the style of coming down, however, remains the most interesting part. She also remembered Hillman as one who until his end created ideas that help us live, and will help us die.

Through *Heartbreak* I understand that loss or heartbreak is an experience of being disconnected from the source of love, security, and acceptance that causes an unbearable psychic pain. When we experience that pain, we easily equate connectedness or love with death—psychic or physical. It is therefore crucial to transform the trauma of heartbreak into a process of an ever-expanding consciousness. It has also been neuro-scientifically proven that our brain has the capacity to do this.

Never fully accepted by my mother as a daughter with a defected left hand and orphaned at a young age, I had the tendency to attach myself to security providers such as teachers, bosses, and superiors easily. Those attachments became strong and deep to the point that I enslaved myself to them. Now I must find and use my own inner authority. I understood from *Heartbreak* that my brain learns by defeat as much as by victory. It reacts as forcefully to placebo (positive suggestion) as well as to nocebo (negative suggestion). I must add that what was missing: the adult writer instead of staring at what should have been; or analyzing the defeat. As Paris would say: "It is not what is there that creates the problem, but what is not there."

Impacted by these sudden deaths of two close friends and inspired by and deeply grateful for 'The Art of Dying' I began to revise my memoir with a new understanding that reaching home is a lifelong, spiraling process that happens over and over again. It's an ever-enlarging awareness. The missing adult writer must be lived.

This type of learning is like the manna which sustained the Israelites in the desert: experiences of disappointment and fulfillment, despair and joy, discouragement and hope—the sustenance that had to be digested and lived. Did it really take that long—forty years—before they got to the promise land?

It has taken me years to fully understand and be wedded to my masculine self, and respect the ecstasy in writing and singing.

I had a ride with Tom to the White Tank Mountain the other day. The weather was so perfect for an outdoor activity. Quite a number of people were out for a hike and/

or a picnic lunch. Tom and I hiked together for a while, took a rest, and then went our different ways. We met at five o'clock on the bench under the blossoming Palo Verdi.

Soon after starting my own walk, an old crooked, burly oak tree stopped me. The deep reaching roots were sturdy, the branches full of budding leaves. It had a few unusually shaped knuckles, strong and shiny. It made me wonder what it had gone through in its younger years. I imagined the tree had survived several heavy storms. One that bent it to one side, another to the opposite side, then back up right again. It stood there gracious, strong and firm, inviting hikers like me admire her. The shiny sturdy roots and the rustling leaves captured my attention. I could not help but think of the old nutmeg tree in front of Grandma's house.

Just behind the tree was a small creek, and along its side was a smooth path. I followed that path for a while, then took a turn, and then another. Somehow I could not find my way back to the bench. I was frustrated and tired. When I finally found the bench under the shady tree, ah, what a relief! Only to find out that Tom too had just arrived. A little dog separated from her family had held him up. Fortunately they were reunited. As usual we reflected on and shared our experiences. Doesn't life include taking byways, being stopped and getting lost?

Filled with humility and joy I re-arranged my writing space, re-read books, designed a new regimen for writing.

Since my hearing and sight began to diminish I stopped singing in the choir. Singing I still do. It was in writing that healing took place and in turn enabled me to discern that what matters most: to discover and express a divine nonchalance—as mentioned by Patricia Hample in *Blue Arabesque*—that deep passion Henri Matisse had for odalisques coupled with the daily strokes of the brush. I treasure the opportunity to express that same ecstasy, the divine nonchalance, in the stillness of the desert: writing combined with the discipline that Grandma had taught me.

Postlude

In deep gratitude I humbly conclude.
The path to ever-widening awareness brings me
to experience and stay in a tension of opposites:
the masculine, the feminine. They transcend.

Upwards, downwards, ever-widening path spirals.
The impossible and unthinkable surprises.
Transcending they are no more this or that alone;
A new creation of dual subjects, they are.

The impossible, the unthinkable is hard to grasp
at first. The simultaneous pull makes me uneasy.
To let the new creation emerge I must listen,
make room for the mystery of life.

Uneasy and insecure to face the unknown
I deeply listen, over and over again.
The mystery that underlies life fills me with joy.
Enriched I add my little share to the whole.

To listen deeply over and over again humbles.
It encourages to love the feminine.
My little share adds to the mosaic of the universe.
Rejoice, rejoice, rejoice the great rebirth.

Encouraged to love the feminine
I experience and stay in a tension of opposites.
It's the story of my grandma's nutmeg tree.
In deep gratitude I humbly conclude.

Acknowledgements

I am filled with gratitude for my circle of friends: writers, poets, ICA friends, Jungian analysts, who have helped conceive, shape the story of my life. Some of you have shared your stories that enriched mine. It broke my heart when two of you passed away and were not there to rejoice its birth. Lovingly and patiently you stood by me as I endured the pangs of giving birth to this memoir. Except for a few, some names mentioned are fictitious.

My appreciation goes to Mel Mathews of Fisher King Press, for his soulful guidance. I am grateful to Charles Mannino for his editorial accuracy and computer expertise. How thankful I am to Wikipedia for historical data made available at our fingertips.

My heartfelt thanks goes to Budhianto Hadinugroho for recovering special family data and photographs and also to Adhi Utomo for editing the pictures.

Made in the USA
Monee, IL
07 July 2026